CONTENTS

Question and answer bank

INTRODUCTION

This is BPP Learning Media's AAT Question Bank for *Bookkeeping Controls*. It is part of a suite of ground-breaking resources produced by BPP Learning Media for AAT assessments.

This Question Bank has been written in conjunction with the BPP Course Book, and has been carefully designed to enable students to practise all of the learning outcomes and assessment criteria for the units that make up *Bookkeeping Controls*. It is fully up to date as at April 2016 and reflects both the AAT's qualification specification and the sample assessment provided by the AAT.

This Question Bank contains these key features:

- Tasks corresponding to each chapter of the Course Book. Some tasks are designed for learning purposes, others are of assessment standard

- AAT's AQ2016 sample assessment and answers for *Bookkeeping Controls* and further BPP practice assessments

The emphasis in all tasks and assessments is on the practical application of the skills acquired.

VAT

You may find tasks throughout this Question Bank that need you to calculate or be aware of a rate of VAT. This is stated at 20% in these examples and questions.

Approaching the assessment

When you sit the assessment it is very important that you follow the on screen instructions. This means you need to carefully read the instructions, both on the introduction screens and during specific tasks.

When you access the assessment you should be presented with an introductory screen with information similar to that shown below (taken from the introductory screen from one of the AAT's AQ2016 Sample Assessments for *Bookkeeping Controls)*.

We have provided the following assessment to help you familiarise yourself with AAT's e-assessment environment. It is designed to demonstrate as many as possible of the question types you may find in a live assessment. It is not designed to be used on its own to determine whether you are ready for a live assessment.

Please note that in this sample test only your responses to tasks 1-5 and 7-9 are marked. Equivalents of tasks 6 and 10 will be human marked in the live assessment.

This assessment contains <u>10 tasks</u> and you should attempt and aim to complete EVERY task. Each task is independent. You will not need to refer to your answers to previous tasks. Read every task carefully to make sure you understand what is required.

Where the date is relevant, it is given in the task data.

Both minus signs and brackets can be used to indicate negative numbers UNLESS task instructions say otherwise.

You must use a full stop to indicate a decimal point. For example, write 100.57 NOT 100,57 or 100 57

You may use a comma to indicate a number in the thousands, but you don't have to. For example, 10000 and 10,000 are both OK.

Other indicators are not compatible with the computer-marked system.

Complete all 10 tasks

The actual instructions will vary depending on the subject you are studying for. It is very important you read the instructions on the introductory screen and apply them in the assessment. You don't want to lose marks when you know the correct answer just because you have not entered it in the right format.

In general, the rules set out in the AAT Sample Assessments for the subject you are studying for will apply in the real assessment, but you should carefully read the information on this screen again in the real assessment, just to make sure. This screen may also confirm the VAT rate used if applicable.

A full stop is needed to indicate a decimal point. We would recommend using minus signs to indicate negative numbers and leaving out the comma signs to indicate thousands, as this results in a lower number of key strokes and less margin for error when working under time pressure. Having said that, you can use whatever is easiest for you as long as you operate within the rules set out for your particular assessment.

You have to show competence throughout the assessment and you should therefore complete all of the tasks. Don't leave questions unanswered.

In some assessments, written or complex tasks may be human marked. In this case you are given a blank space or table to enter your answer into. You are told in the assessments which tasks these are (note: there may be none if all answers are marked by the computer).

If these involve calculations, it is a good idea to decide in advance how you are going to lay out your answers to such tasks by practising answering them on a word document, and certainly you should try all such tasks in this Question Bank and in the AAT's environment using the sample assessment.

When asked to fill in tables, or gaps, never leave any blank even if you are unsure of the answer. Fill in your best estimate.

Note that for some assessments where there is a lot of scenario information or tables of data provided (eg tax tables), you may need to access these via 'pop-ups'. Instructions will be provided on how you can bring up the necessary data during the assessment.

Finally, take note of any task specific instructions once you are in the assessment. For example you may be asked to enter a date in a certain format or to enter a number to a certain number of decimal places.

Grading

To achieve the qualification and to be awarded a grade, you must pass all the mandatory unit assessments, all optional unit assessments (where applicable) and the synoptic assessment.

The AAT Level 2 Foundation Certificate in Accounting will be awarded a grade. This grade will be based on performance across the qualification. Unit assessments and synoptic assessments are not individually graded. These assessments are given a mark that is used in calculating the overall grade.

How overall grade is determined

You will be awarded an overall qualification grade (Distinction, Merit, and Pass). If you do not achieve the qualification you will not receive a qualification certificate, and the grade will be shown as unclassified.

The marks of each assessment will be converted into a percentage mark and rounded up or down to the nearest whole number. This percentage mark is then weighted according to the weighting of the unit assessment or synoptic assessment within the qualification. The resulting weighted assessment percentages are combined to arrive at a percentage mark for the whole qualification.

Grade definition	Percentage threshold
Distinction	90–100%
Merit	80–89%
Pass	70–79%
Unclassified	0–69%
	Or failure to pass one or more assessment/s

Re-sits

Some AAT qualifications such as the AAT Foundation Certificate in Accounting have restrictions in place for how many times you are able to re-sit assessments. Please refer to the AAT website for further details.

You should only be entered for an assessment when you are well prepared and you expect to pass the assessment.

AAT qualifications

The material in this book may support the following AAT qualifications:

AAT Foundation Certificate in Accounting Level 2, AAT Foundation Certificate in Accounting at SCQF Level 5 and Certificate: Accounting Technician (Level 3 AATSA).

Supplements

From time to time we may need to publish supplementary materials to one of our titles. This can be for a variety of reasons. From a small change in the AAT unit guidance to new legislation coming into effect between editions.

You should check our supplements page regularly for anything that may affect your learning materials. All supplements are available free of charge on our supplements page on our website at:

www.bpp.com/learning-media/about/students

Improving material and removing errors

There is a constant need to update and enhance our study materials in line with both regulatory changes and new insights into the assessments.

From our team of authors BPP appoints a subject expert to update and improve these materials for each new edition.

Their updated draft is subsequently technically checked by another author and from time to time non-technically checked by a proof reader.

We are very keen to remove as many numerical errors and narrative typos as we can but given the volume of detailed information being changed in a short space of time we know that a few errors will sometimes get though our net.

We apologise in advance for any inconvenience that an error might cause. We continue to look for new ways to improve these study materials and would welcome your suggestions. If you have any comments about this book, please email nisarahmed@bpp.com or write to Nisar Ahmed, AAT Head of Programme, BPP Learning Media Ltd, BPP House, Aldine Place, London W12 8AA.

Question bank

Bookkeeping Controls Question bank

Chapter 1 Payment Methods

Task 1.1

Given below are four cheques received by Southfield Electrical today, 9 January 20X6.

Check each one thoroughly and identify the error on the cheques below, selecting your answer from the picklist.

	Comments	
Cheque from B B Berry Ltd		▼
Cheque from Q Q Stores		▼
Cheque from Dagwell Enterprises		▼
Cheque from Weller Enterprises		▼

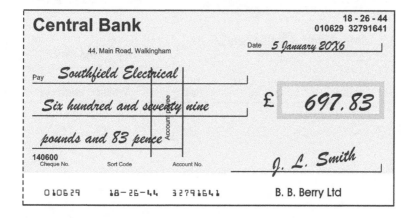

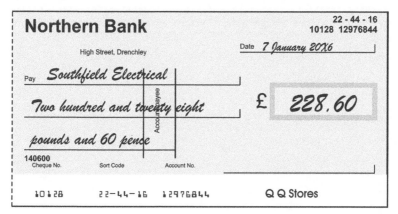

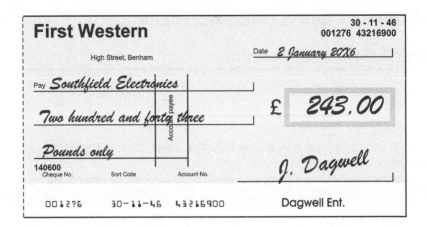

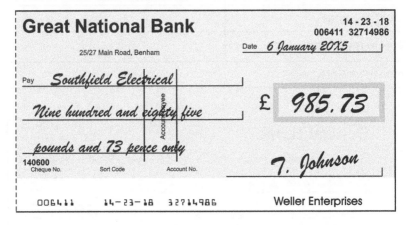

Picklist

Amount
Date
Payee
Signature

....

4

Task 1.2

Frank Limited needs to make several payments to its suppliers. **Select the correct payment method in each case from the picklist provided. You may use the same option more than once.**

Situation	Payment method
Payment to Kim Guitars Ltd for £2,500 for items purchased on credit. The payment is required within 5 days	▼
Payment of £1,000 to Pixie Bass as a deposit on a supply. The payment is required today to release the shipment	▼
Payment of £265,000 to Paz Ltd to secure a new retail unit. Immediate payment is required	▼
Payment to Santiago Strings for £875 to pay an invoice due by the end of the week	▼

Picklist

BACS Direct Credit
CHAPS
Faster Payment

Task 1.3

Complete the following statements by selecting the relevant banking terms from the picklist.

(a) A [   ] would be set up to repay a bank loan in equal monthly instalments.

(b) A [   ] would be set up to make the minimum payment on a credit card by variable amounts each month.

(c) A bank [   ] would be arranged when short-term borrowing is needed.

Picklist

direct debit
overdraft
standing order

Task 1.4

Using the picklist, select the most suitable payment method for each of the business expenses.

Situation	Solution
Making regular rent payments	▼
Purchase of office stationery online	▼
Payment of wages to staff	▼
Payment of £2,500 to a supplier after taking 15 days credit	▼
Buying tea bags for the office	▼
Payment of £375 for new tyres for the company van	▼

Picklist

BACS direct credit
Bank draft
Cash
Debit card
Standing order

Task 1.5

Which TWO of the following items should be checked when a cheque is accepted as payment from customers?

	✓
Funds are available in customer's account	
Issue number	
Words and figures match	
Security number	
Expiry date	
Date is not in the future	

Task 1.6

The director of Parker Flooring Limited has made a number of payments today (2 February 20X6) in respect of materials for the company. **Select the correct impact on the bank account from the picklist below.**

Payment	Impact on the bank account
Cheque written for £550 to Soft Carpets Limited	▼
Debit card to buy diesel for the van £65	▼
Credit card to buy printer cartridges online £30	▼
Payment of a purchase invoice using BACS direct credit to Solvit Limited £1,200	▼
Cheque written for £276 to Wall2Wall Limited	▼
Debit card to buy coffee from the local store of £5.67	▼
Bank draft for £10,000 to purchase a new van	▼

Picklist

Delayed
Immediate (within 24 hours)

Task 1.7

Given below is a completed cheque. Complete the following statements by selecting from the picklist

Who is the drawee?	▼
Who is the payee?	▼
Who is the drawer?	▼

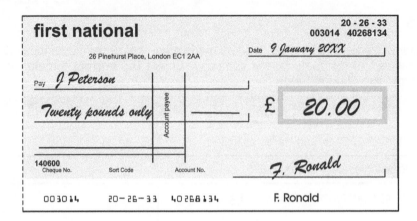

Picklist

F Ronald
First National
J Peterson

Chapter 2 Bank reconciliations

Task 2.1

Would each of the following transactions appear as a payment in or a payment out on a business's bank statement?

Transaction	Payment out ✓	Payment in ✓
£470.47 paid into the bank		
Standing order of £26.79		
Cheque payment of £157.48		
Interest earned on the bank balance		
BACS payment for wages		

Task 2.2

You are given information about Newmans' receipts during the week ending 27 January. They represent payments by credit customers and receipts for sales to non-credit customers of music, instruments and CDs which were settled by cheque.

Details		Amount £
Tunfield DC	Bank transfer	594.69
Tunshire County Orchestra	Bank transfer	468.29
Sale of music	Cheque	478.90
Tunfield Brass Band	Credit	1,059.72
Sale of instruments	Cheque	752.16
Sale of CDs	Cheque	256.80

You need to update the cash book to reflect the impact of these receipts

(a) **Enter the correct entries from the picklist provided and total the debit side of the cash book given below:**

Cash book – debit side

Date	Details	Bank £
	Bal b/f	379.22
	▼	
	▼	
	▼	
	▼	
	▼	
	▼	
	TOTAL	

Picklist

Non-credit sales
Tunfield BB
Tunfield DC
Tunshire CO

Given below is the credit side of the cash book for Newmans for the week ending 27 January.

Cash book – credit side

Date	Cheque no	Details	Bank £
27 Jan	003014	Henson Press	329.00
27 Jan	003015	Ely Instr	736.96
27 Jan	003016	Jester Press	144.67
27 Jan	003017	CD Supplies	74.54
27 Jan	003018	Jester Press	44.79
27 Jan	003019	Buser Ltd	273.48
27 Jan	SO	Rates	255.00
27 Jan	DD	Rent	500.00

Given below is the bank statement for Newmans for the week ending 27 January.

STATEMENT

first national
26 Pinehurst Place
London
EC1 2AA

NEWMANS

CURRENT ACCOUNT

Account number: 40268134

Sheet 023

Date		Paid out	Paid in	Balance
20XX				
20 Jan	Balance b/f			379.22 CR
24 Jan	Counter credit – Tunfield		594.69	
	Counter credit – Tunshire Co		468.29	
24 Jan	SO – British Elec	212.00		1,230.20 CR
25 Jan	Counter credit – Tunfield AOS		108.51	1,338.71 CR
26 Jan	Cheque No 003014	329.00		
	Credit		478.90	1,488.61 CR
27 Jan	Cheque No 003017	74.54		
	Cheque No 003015	736.96		
	Credit		1,059.72	
	Credit		752.16	
	SO – TDC	255.00		
	DD – Halpern Properties	500.00		
	Bank interest		3.68	1,737.67 CR

(b) Compare the two sides of the cash book from the information given in part (a) to the bank statement. Note any unmatched items below by selecting items from the picklist below and state whether the item needs including in the cash book or in the bank reconciliation.

Unmatched item	£	Action to be taken
▼		▼
▼		▼
▼		▼
▼		▼
▼		▼
▼		▼
▼		▼

Picklist

Bank charge
Bank credit
Bank interest received
Cheque 003016
Cheque 003018
Cheque 003019
Include on bank reconciliation
Sales of CDs
Standing order British Elec
Update cash book

(c) **Using the information available from parts (a) and (b) earlier in this task, consider the required amendments to both sides of the cash book using the picklist provided and enter the balance on the cash book as at 27 January.**

Cash book

Date	Details	Bank £	Cheque number	Details	Bank £
	Balance b/f	379.22	003014	Henson Press	329.00
27 Jan	Tunfield DC	594.69	003015	Ely Instr	736.96
27 Jan	Tunshire CO	468.29	003016	Jester Press	144.67
27 Jan	Non-credit sales	478.90	003017	CD Supplies	74.54
27 Jan	Tunfield BB	1,059.72	003018	Jester Press	44.79
27 Jan	Non-credit sales	752.16	003019	Buser Ltd	273.48
27 Jan	Non-credit sales	256.80	SO	Rates	255.00
27 Jan	▼		DD	Rent	500.00
27 Jan	▼			▼	
				▼	
	Total			Total	

Picklist

Balance b/f
Balance c/d
Bank charges
Bank interest
Standing order
Tunfield AOS
Tunfield DC

(d) Identify the FOUR reconciling items below to prepare the bank reconciliation statement as at 27 January.

Bank reconciliation statement		£
Balance as per bank statement		
Add:		
	▼	
	▼	
Total to add		
Less:		
	▼	
	▼	
	▼	
Total to subtract		
Balance as per cash book		

Task 2.3

On 28 November The Flower Chain received the following bank statement.

High Street Bank plc
The Concourse, Badley, B72 5DG

To: The Flower Chain   Account no: 28710191   Date: 25 November

Statement of Account

Date	Details	Paid out £	Paid in £	Balance £
03 Nov	Balance b/f			9,136 C
07 Nov	Cheque 110870	6,250		2,886 C
17 Nov	Cheque 110872	2,250		636 C
21 Nov	Cheque 110865	3,670		3,034 D
	Direct Debit – Insurance Ensured	500		3,534 D
21 Nov	Counter Credit – BBT Ltd		10,000	6,466 C
24 Nov	Counter credit – Petals Ltd		2,555	9,021 C
	Direct Debit – Rainbow Ltd	88		8,933 C
25 Nov	Cheque 110871	1,164		7,769 C

D = Debit C = Credit

The cash book as at 28 November is shown below.

Cash book

Date	Details	Bank £	Date	Cheque number	Details	Bank £
01 Nov	Balance b/f	5,466	03 Nov	110870	Roberts & Co	6,250
24 Nov	Bevan & Co	1,822	03 Nov	110871	J Jones	1,164
24 Nov	Plant Pots Ltd	7,998	06 Nov	110872	Lake Walks Ltd	2,250
	▼		10 Nov	110873	PH Supplies	275
	▼		17 Nov	110874	Peters & Co	76
					▼	
					▼	
					▼	
	Total				Total	
	▼					

Picklist

Balance b/d
Balance c/d
BBT Ltd
Insurance Ensured
Petals Ltd
Peters & Co
Rainbow Ltd

(a) **Match the items on the bank statement against the items in the cash book.**

(b) **Update the cash book as needed using the picklist and entering the cheque or reference details, plus the amount.**

(c) **Total the cash book and clearly show the balance carried down at 28 November AND brought down at 29 November.**

(d) **Using the picklist provided, identify the FOUR transactions that are included in the cash book but missing from the bank statement and complete the bank reconciliation statement as at 28 November.**

Bank reconciliation statement as at 28 November	£
Balance as per bank statement	
Add:	
Total to add	
Less:	
Total to subtract	
Balance as per cash book	

Picklist

Bevan & Co
Peters & Co
PH Supplies
Plant Pots Ltd

....

Task 2.4

(a) **Which TWO of the following items reconciling the cash book to the bank statement are referred to as timing differences? Tick the appropriate box in the table below.**

	Timing difference? ✓
Bank charges not recorded in the cash book	
Outstanding lodgements	
Interest charged not recorded in the cash book	
Unpresented cheques	

(b) Your cash book at 31 December shows a bank balance of £565 overdrawn. On comparing this with your bank statement at the same date, you discover the following:

A cheque for £57 drawn by you on 29 December has not yet been presented for payment.

A cheque for £92 from a customer, which was paid into the bank on 24 December, has been dishonoured on 31 December.

The correct cash book balance at 31 December is:

	✓
£714 overdrawn	
£657 overdrawn	
£473 overdrawn	
£530 overdrawn	

(c) The cash book shows a bank balance of £5,675 overdrawn at 31 August. It is subsequently discovered that a standing order for £125 has been entered in the cash book twice, and that a dishonoured cheque for £450 has been debited in the cash book instead of credited.

Select the correct bank balance:

	✓
£5,100 overdrawn	
£6,000 overdrawn	
£6,250 overdrawn	
£6,450 overdrawn	

Task 2.5

(a) Your firm's cash book at 30 April shows a balance at the bank of £2,490. Comparison with the bank statement at the same date reveals the following differences:

Transactions	Amount £
Unpresented cheques	840
Bank charges	50
Receipts not yet credited by the bank	470
Dishonoured cheque from customer	140

Select the correct balance on the cash book at 30 April:

	✓
£1,460	
£2,300	
£2,580	
£3,140	

(b) The bank statement at 31 December 20X1 shows a balance of £1,000. The cash book shows a balance of £750.

Which of the following is the most likely reason for the difference?

	✓
Receipts of £250 recorded in the cash book, but not yet recorded by bank	
Bank charges of £250 shown on the bank statement, not in the cash book	
Standing orders of £250 included on bank statement, not in the cash book	
Cheques issued for £250 recorded in the cash book, but not yet gone through the bank account	

(c) Your firm's cash book at 30 April shows a balance at the bank of £3,526. Comparison with the bank statement at the same date reveals the following differences:

	£
Unpresented cheques	920
Bank interest received not in cash book	150
Uncredited lodgements	270
Dishonoured customer's cheque	310

The correct cash book balance at 30 April is:

£ _____

Task 2.6

On 26 July Ottaways Ltd received the following bank statement from Ronda Bank as at 23 July.

Assume today's date is 28 July.

Ronda Bank PLC

Bank Buildings, Flitweck, FT87 1XQ

To: Ottaways Ltd Account No 56235472 23 July

Bank Statement

Date	Detail	Paid out	Paid in	Balance	
20XX		£	£	£	
03 Jul	Balance b/f			1,855	C
03 Jul	Cheque 126459	3,283		1,428	D
03 Jul	Cheque 126460	1,209		2,637	D
03 Jul	Cheque 126461	4,221		6,858	D
04 Jul	Cheque 126464	658		7,516	D
09 Jul	Counter credit SnipSnap Co		8,845	1,329	C
11 Jul	Cheque 126462	1,117		212	C
11 Jul	Direct Debit Flit DC	500		288	D
18 Jul	Direct Debit Consol Landlords	475		763	D
20 Jul	Bank Charges	32		795	D
22 Jul	Interest for month	103		898	D
23 Jul	Counter credit		5,483	4,585	C

D = Debit C = Credit

The cash book as at 23 July is shown below.

(a) **Match the items on the bank statement against the items in the cash book.**

(b) **Using the picklist below for the details column, enter any items in the cash book as needed.**

(c) **Total the cash book and clearly show the balance carried down at 23 July and brought down at 24 July.**

(d) **Using the picklist below, complete the bank reconciliation statement as at 23 July.**

Cash book

Date	Details	Bank £	Date	Cheque number	Details	Bank £
01 Jul	Balance b/f	1,855	01 Jul	126459	Gumpley Co	3,283
20 Jul	Brimfull Ltd	5,483	01 Jul	126460	Warnes Ltd	1,209
21 Jul	Adera Ltd	2,198	01 Jul	126461	Veldt Partners	4,221
22 Jul	Mist Northern	1,004	01 Jul	126462	Pathways	1,117
	▼		02 Jul	126463	Lindstrom Co	846
			02 Jul	126464	Kestrels Training	658
			13 Jul	126465	HGW Ltd	3,200
			13 Jul		Flit DC	500
					▼	
					▼	
					▼	
					▼	
	Total				Total	
	▼					

Bank reconciliation statement as at 23 July	£
Balance per bank statement	
Add:	
▼	
▼	
Total to add	
Less:	
▼	
▼	
Total to subtract	
Balance as per cash book	

Picklist

Adera Ltd
Balance b/d
Balance c/d
Bank charges
Brimfull Ltd
Consol Landlords
Flit DC
Gumpley Co
HGW Ltd
Interest
Kestrels Training
Lindstrom Co
Mist Northern
Pathways
SnipSnap Co
Veldt Partners
Warnes Ltd

Chapter 3 Introduction to control accounts

Task 3.1

Assuming they all <u>include VAT</u> where relevant, identify the double entry for the following transactions.

Here is a list of the transactions for August 20XX

Transactions	Amount £
Credit purchases	3,390
Credit sales returns	1,860
Payments to credit suppliers	4,590
Receipts from credit customers	5,480
Discounts allowed	400
Discounts received	200

Show the journal entries needed to record the following:

(a) Purchases

Account		Amount £	Debit	Credit
	▼			
	▼			
	▼			

(b) Sales returns

Account		Amount £	Debit	Credit
	▼			
	▼			
	▼			

(c) Payments to credit suppliers

Account	Amount £	Debit	Credit
▼			
▼			

(d) Receipts from credit customers

Account	Amount £	Debit	Credit
▼			
▼			

Picklist

Bank
Discounts allowed
Discounts received
Purchase ledger control
Purchases
Sales ledger control
Sales returns
VAT control a/c

··

Task 3.2

Your organisation is not registered for VAT. The balance on the sales ledger control account on 1 January was £11,689. The transactions that take place during January are summarised below:

Transactions	Amount £
Credit sales	12,758
Sales returns	1,582
Cash received from trade receivables	11,563
Discounts allowed	738

You are required to write up the sales ledger control account using the picklist below for the month of January.

Sales ledger control

Details		Amount £	Details		Amount £
	▼			▼	
	▼			▼	
				▼	
				▼	

Picklist

Balance b/f
Balance c/d
Bank
Discounts allowed
Sales
Sales returns

Task 3.3

Your organisation is not registered for VAT. The opening balance on the purchases ledger control account at 1 January was £8,347. The transactions for the month of January have been summarised below:

Transactions	Amount £
Credit purchases	9,203
Purchases returns	728
Payments to trade payables	8,837
Discounts received	382

You are required to write up the purchases ledger control account for the month of January.

Purchases ledger control

Details		Amount £	Details		Amount £
	▼		Balance b/f		
	▼			▼	
	▼				
	▼				

Picklist

Balance c/d
Bank
Discounts received
Purchases
Purchases returns

Task 3.4

This is a summary of transactions with credit suppliers during June.

Transactions	Amount £
Balance of trade payables at 1 June	85,299
Goods bought on credit – gross	39,300
Payments made to credit suppliers	33,106
Discounts received	1,000
Goods returned to credit suppliers – gross	275

Prepare a purchases ledger control account from the details shown above. Show clearly the balance carried down at 30 June AND brought down at 1 July.

Purchases ledger control account

Date	Details	Amount £	Date	Details	Amount £
	▼			Balance b/f	
	▼			▼	
	▼				
	▼				
				▼	

Picklist

Balance b/d
Balance c/d
Bank
Discounts received
Purchases
Purchases returns

....

Task 3.5

(a) The sales ledger control account at 1 May had a balance of £31,475. During May, gross sales of £125,000 were made on credit. Receipts from trade receivables amounted to £122,500 and discounts of £550 were allowed. Credit notes of £1,300 gross were issued to customers.

The closing balance at 31 May is:

£32,125	
£33,975	
£34,725	
£33,225	

(b) Your purchases ledger control account has a balance at 1 October of £34,500 credit. During October, gross credit purchases were £78,400, gross cash purchases were £2,400 and payments made to suppliers, excluding cash purchases, and after deducting settlement discounts of £1,200, were £68,900. Gross purchases returns were £4,700.

The closing balance was:

	✓
£38,100	
£40,500	
£47,500	
£49,900	

Task 3.6

Sunshine Limited has calculated its VAT for the month of March. It has a VAT control account credit balance of £4,500 brought down on 1 March 20XX.

There are a number of transactions made during the month.

Details	Amount £
VAT on sales	6,000
VAT on sales returns	300
VAT on purchases	2,500
Bank payment made to HMRC	7,000
VAT on purchases returns	250

(a) Prepare the VAT control account for March 20XX. Show the balance c/d at 31 March 20XX and the balance b/d at 1 April 20XX.

Details	Amount £	Details	Amount £
▼		Balance b/f	4,500
▼		▼	
▼		▼	
▼			
		▼	

Picklist

Balance b/d
Balance b/f
Balance c/d
Payment to HMRC
VAT on purchases
VAT on purchase returns
VAT on sales
VAT on sales returns

(b) If the VAT of £4,500 calculated on sales made by Sunshine Limited during April 20XX, and there were no other VAT transactions, what would be the liability to HMRC at 30 April 20XX?

£ [　　　　　]

Chapter 4 Preparing and reconciling control accounts

Task 4.1

When reconciling sales ledger and purchases ledger control accounts to the list of balances from the subsidiary ledgers, would the following errors affect the relevant control account, the list of balances or both?

	Control account ✓	List of balances ✓	Both ✓
Invoice entered into the sales day book as £980 instead of £890			
Purchases day book overcast by £1,000			
Discounts allowed of £20 not entered into the cash book (debit side)			
An invoice taken as £340 instead of £440 when being posted to the customer's account			
Incorrect balancing of a memorandum ledger account			
A purchases return not entered into the purchases returns day book			

Task 4.2

James has just completed his first month of trading. James makes sales on credit to four customers and the transactions during his second month of trading were as follows. James is not registered for VAT.

Transactions	Amount £
Sales to H Simms	2,000
Sales to P Good	2,700
Sales to K Mitchell	1,100
Sales to C Brown	3,800
Receipt from H Simms	2,400
Receipts from P Good	3,600
Receipts from K Mitchell	1,100
Receipts from C Brown	4,800

You are required to:

(a) **Using the picklist below, show these transactions in total in the sales ledger control account and in detail in the individual sales ledger accounts. Each of the accounts shows, where appropriate, the opening balance at the start of the second month.**

(b) **Balance the sales ledger control account and the individual sales ledger accounts.**

(c) **Reconcile the list of sales ledger balances to the balance on the control account.**

Sales ledger control account

Details	Amount £	Details	Amount £
Balance b/f	5,000	▾	
▾		▾	
▾			

Sales ledger

H Simms

Details	Amount £	Details	Amount £
Balance b/f	900	▼	
▼		▼	
▼		▼	

P Good

Details	Amount £	Details	Amount £
Balance b/f	1,600	▼	
▼		▼	
▼			

K Mitchell

Details	Amount £	Details	Amount £
▼		▼	

C Brown

Details	Amount £	Details	Amount £
Balance b/f	2,500	▼	
▼		▼	
▼			

Reconciliation of sales ledger balances with the control account balance

	£
H Simms	
P Good	
K Mitchell	
C Brown	
Sales ledger control account	

Picklist

Balance b/d
Balance c/d
Bank
Sales

Task 4.3

James also buys goods on credit from three suppliers. The transactions with these suppliers in month two are summarised below. James is not registered for VAT.

Transactions	Amount £
Purchase from J Peters	1,600
Purchase from T Sands	2,500
Purchase from L Farmer	3,200

Transactions	Amount £
Payment to J Peters	1,700
Payment to T Sands	3,200
Payment to L Farmer	3,000

You are required to:

(a) **Using the picklist below, show these transactions in total in the purchases ledger control account and in detail in the individual purchases ledger accounts. Each of the accounts shows, where appropriate, the opening balance at the start of the second month.**

(b) **Balance the purchases ledger control account and the individual purchases ledger accounts.**

(c) Reconcile the list of purchases ledger balances to the balance on the control account.

Picklist

Bank
Purchases
Balance b/d
Balance c/d

Purchases ledger control account

Details	Amount £	Details	Amount £
▼		Balance b/f	2,700
▼		▼	
		▼	

Purchases ledger

J Peters

Details	Amount £	Details	Amount £
▼		Balance b/f	300
▼		▼	
		▼	

T Sands

Details	Amount £	Details	Amount £
▼		Balance b/f	1,700
▼		▼	
		▼	

33

L Farmer

Details	Amount £	Details	Amount £
		Balance b/f	700
▼		▼	
		▼	

Reconciliation of purchases ledger balances with control account balance

	£
J Peters	
T Sands	
L Farmer	
Purchases ledger control account	

Task 4.4

The following are the sales ledger transactions for June 20XX

Transactions	Amount £
Items sold on credit	14,500
Returns from customers	700
Receipts from customers	15,600

(a) **You are required to write up the sales ledger control account. Please use the picklist provided:**

Sales ledger control

Details	Amount £	Details	Amount £
Balance b/f	9,450	▾	
▾		▾	
		▾	
▾			

Picklist

Balance b/d
Balance c/d
Bank
Sales on credit
Returns

The following are the balances on the sales ledger.

Details	Amount £
Annabel Limited	3,000
Bahira Limited	1,250
Clara Limited	3,310

(b) **What is the difference between the sales ledger control account and the sales ledger?**

£ [   ]

(c) **Which TWO of the following reasons could explain why there is this difference between the sales ledger control account and the sales ledger?**

Reasons	
A cash receipt was incorrectly entered onto the customer's account in the sales ledger	☐
A sales invoice has been duplicated in the sales ledger	☐
A sales return credit note has only been recorded in the sales ledger control account	☐
Discounts have been posted twice in the customer's sales ledger account	☐

Task 4.5

The following is an extract of the balances on the purchase ledger as at 31 July 20XX

Transactions	Amount £
Goods purchased on credit during July	8,600
Payments made to credit suppliers in July	9,750
Discounts received	500

The brought forward balance at 1 July 20XX was £12,500

(a) **Complete the purchase ledger control account using the balances above. Remember to calculate the balance brought down at 1 August 20XX.**

Purchase ledger control

Details	Amount £	Details	Amount £
▼		Balance b/f	
▼		▼	
▼			
		▼	

Picklist

Balance b/d
Balance c/d
Bank
Discounts received
Purchases

The following are the balances on the purchase ledger as at 31 July 20XX:

Purchase ledger

Transactions	Amount £
Cargo Transport Limited	5,400
Utilities Financing Limited	1,200
Airborne Parcels Limited	2,000
LoGist Limited	1,250
Wrap Around Limited	800

(b) Using the information from the purchase ledger in part (a), complete the purchase ledger account reconciliation in the table below

	£
Purchase ledger control account balance as at 31 July 20XX	
Total of the purchase ledger accounts as at 31 July 20XX	
Difference	

(c) Select the ONE correct possible reason for this difference on the purchase ledger reconciliation

Reason	
Purchases on credit have been recorded on the debit side of the purchase ledger	☐
A purchase invoice has been duplicated in the purchase ledger	☐
Discounts received have been omitted from the purchases ledger but recorded in the purchases ledger control account	☐
A cash payment to a credit supplier has been recorded in the purchase ledger control account only	☐

Task 4.6

This is a summary of your business's transactions with credit customers during November.

	£
Balance of trade receivables at 1 November	48,125
Goods sold on credit (gross value)	37,008
Money received from credit customers	28,327
Discounts allowed	240
Goods returned by customers (gross value)	2,316

(a) Using the picklist provided below, prepare a sales ledger control account from the details shown above. Show clearly the balance carried down at 30 November AND brought down at 1 December.

Sales ledger control

Date	Details	Amount £	Date	Details		Amount £
	Balance b/f				▼	
	▼				▼	
					▼	
					▼	
	▼					

Picklist

Balance b/d
Balance b/f
Balance c/d
Bank
Discounts allowed
Sales
Sales returns

The following balances were in the sales ledger on 1 December:

Transactions	Amount £
J Hicks Ltd	3,298
Parks and Gardens	4,109
Greener Grass	18,250
TTL Ltd	18,106
Reeves and Wright	10,400

(b) Reconcile the balances shown above with the sales ledger control account balance you have calculated in part (a).

Sales ledger control account balance as at 1 December	
Total of sales ledger accounts as at 1 December	
Difference	

(c) Because of an error in the sales ledger, there is a difference. What might have caused the difference? Tick TWO reasons only.

	✓
VAT has been overstated on an invoice.	
VAT has been understated on an invoice.	
A sales invoice has been entered in the sales ledger twice.	
A sales credit note has been entered in the sales ledger twice.	
A receipt from a customer has been omitted from the sales ledger.	
A receipt from a customer has been entered in the sales ledger twice.	

Task 4.7

The following transactions take place during a three month period

(a) Calculate the VAT on the balances and complete the table below (round your answers to the nearest pound).

Transactions	Amount £	VAT £
Sales on credit including VAT at 20%	106,800	
Purchases on credit including VAT at 20%	54,000	
Credit notes issued including VAT at 20%	2,820	

(b) Using the VAT figures calculated above, complete the VAT control account, including the balance brought down at the end of the quarter. Use the picklist provided.

VAT control

Details	Amount £	Details	Amount £
▼		▼	
▼			
▼			
		▼	

Picklist

Balance b/d
Balance c/d
Purchases
Sales
Sales returns

(c) **The amount payable to HMRC for the quarter will be**

£	

Task 4.8

At the end of the last VAT period, the VAT account for Fast Fashions showed that a refund was due from HM Revenue & Customs.

(a) **Select ONE reason that would cause a refund to be due to Fast Fashions.**

The sales ledger control account shows a difference to the sales ledger account balances	
Sales were less than purchases for the quarter	
There was an underpayment of VAT in the previous quarter	

Sales in June totalled £129,240, all including VAT.

(b) **What is the amount of output VAT on sales?**

£	

Task 4.9

(a) A supplier sends you a statement showing a balance outstanding of £14,350. Your own records show a balance outstanding of £14,500.

The reason for this difference could be that

	✓
The supplier sent an invoice for £150 which you have not yet received	
The supplier has allowed you £150 settlement discount which you had not entered in your ledger	
You have paid the supplier £150 which he has not yet accounted for	
You have returned goods worth £150 which the supplier has not yet accounted for	

(b) An invoice for £69 has been recorded in the sales day book as £96.

When the sales ledger reconciliation is prepared, adjustments will be required to:

	✓
The control account only	
The list of balances only	
Both the control account and the list of balances	

At the end of the month, the purchase ledger control account has credit entries amounting to £76,961 and debit balances amounting to £24,500.

The following transactions need to be recorded in the purchase ledger control account:

- Correction of a duplicated supplier's invoice for £4,688
- Standing order payments to suppliers of £1,606

(c) **What will be the corrected purchase ledger control account balance brought down after the transactions above have been recorded? Tick the correct entry to show whether this balance will be a debit or a credit.**

Amount £	Debit ✓	Credit ✓

Task 4.10

(a) You have been handed an aged receivable analysis which shows a total balance of £109,456.

This amount should reconcile with which TWO of the following?

	✓
The balance on the bank statement	
The balance on the sales ledger control account	
The balance on the purchases ledger control account	
The total of all the purchases ledger balances	
The total of all the sales ledger balances	

(b) Complete the following sentence:

The aged receivable analysis shows:

	✓
How much is owed to suppliers at any point	
Over how many months the outstanding balance owed by each individual credit customer has built up	
The total purchases over the year to date to each credit supplier	

Task 4.11

A credit customer, B B Brand Ltd, has ceased trading, owing Kitchen Kuts £1,560 plus VAT.

(a) Record the journal entries needed in the general ledger to write off the net amount and the VAT.

Account name		Amount £	Debit ✓	Credit ✓
	▼			
	▼			
	▼			

Picklist

Irrecoverable debts

Sales ledger control

VAT control

Kitchen Kuts has the following transactions for the month (all figures include VAT):

- Credit sales of £8,400
- Purchases of £540
- Sales returns of £300

(b) Record the transactions above in the VAT control account, including the entries for the irrecoverable debt of B B Brand Ltd and the VAT brought down figure for the following month. Use the picklist provided.

VAT control account

Details	Amount £	Details	Amount £
		Balance b/f	250
▼		▼	
▼			
▼			
▼	=====		=====
	=====		=====
		▼	

Picklist

Balance b/d
Balance c/d
Irrecoverable debt expense
Purchases
Sales
Sales returns

Task 4.12

A credit customer, ABC Ltd, has ceased trading, owing your firm £240 plus VAT.

Prepare a journal to write off the net amount and VAT in the general ledger.

Journal

Account name	Amount £	Debit ✓	Credit ✓
▼			
▼			
▼			

Picklist

Irrecoverable debt expense
Sales ledger control
VAT control

Task 4.13

Textile Carpets has a credit customer, Flooring King, who has ceased trading, owing the business £2,370. Textile Carpets is registered for VAT at 20%

Record the journal entries needed in the general ledger to write off the net amount and the VAT.

Account name		Amount £	Debit ✓	Credit ✓
	▼			
	▼			
	▼			

Picklist

Irrecoverable debt expense
Sales ledger control
VAT control

Chapter 5 The journal

Task 5.1

An organisation has started a new business and a new set of accounts is to be opened. The opening balances for the new business are as follows:

Details	Amount £
Capital	10,000
Furniture and fittings	15,315
Motor vehicles	20,109
Cash at bank	15,000
Purchase ledger control	37,238
Sales ledger control	12,524
Loan from bank	7,000
VAT (owed to HM Revenue & Customs)	8,710

Using the picklist below, prepare a journal to enter these opening balances into the accounts.

Journal

Account name		Debit £	Credit £
	▼		
	▼		
	▼		
	▼		
	▼		
	▼		
	▼		
	▼		
Totals			

Picklist

Capital
Cash at bank
Furniture and fittings
Loan from bank

Motor vehicles
Purchases ledger control
Sales ledger control
VAT control (owed to HM Revenue & Customs)

Task 5.2

A new business has already started to trade, though it is not yet registered for VAT, and now wishes to open up its first set of accounts. You are handed the following information:

	£
Bank	300
Petty cash	200
Trade receivables	7,700
Bank loan	9,000
VAT	1,300
Trade creditors	3,400
Van	6,000
Capital	500

Record the journal entries needed in the accounts in the general ledger of the business to deal with the opening entries. Use the picklist below to select your account, write in the amount to be entered and tick the appropriate entry to show whether a debit or a credit.

Account name	Amount £	Debit ✓	Credit ✓
▼			
▼			
▼			
▼			
▼			
▼			
▼			
▼			

Picklist

Bank
Capital
Loan from bank
Petty cash
Trade creditors
Trade receivables
Van
VAT control

Task 5.3

Kitchen Kuts has started a new business, Kitchen Capers, and a new set of accounts is to be opened. A partially completed journal to record the opening entries is shown below.

Record the journal entries needed in the accounts in the general ledger of Kitchen Capers to deal with the opening entries.

Account name	Amount £	Debit ✓	Credit ✓
Cash	150		
Cash at bank	12,350		
Capital	23,456		
Fixtures and Fittings	2,100		
Trade receivables	3,206		
Loan from bank	10,000		
Motor vehicle	15,650		

Task 5.4

Peter Knight is one of the employees at Short Furniture. The payroll department have calculated his payroll for May as follows.

Details	Amount £
Gross salary	2,200
National Insurance Contributions (Employee)	183
National Insurance Contributions (Employer)	200
Income Tax	256

(a) Calculate Peter's net salary for the month.

£ _____

(b) Show how all of the elements of Peter's salary including the net salary as shown in part (a) would be entered into the accounting records by using the picklist below and writing up the ledger accounts given.

Salary expense

Details	Amount £	Details	Amount £
▼			
▼			

Salary control

Details	Amount £	Details	Amount £
▼		▼	
▼		▼	
▼			
▼			

HMRC control

Details	Amount £	Details	Amount £
		▼	
		▼	
		▼	

Bank

Details	Amount £	Details	Amount £
		▼	

Picklist

Bank
HMRC control
Salary control
Salary expense

Task 5.5

Select the correct recipient of each of the following payroll related costs

Income tax	Employee

NIC (employee)	HMRC

Pension contributions	Pension company

Net salary	Employer

Task 5.6

Georgia Blossom has her monthly salary paid to her on the 28th of the month. She pays into the pension scheme and her employer contributes an additional 4% of her gross salary as pension contributions.

These are the calculations for Georgia's August 20XX salary.

	Amount £
Gross Salary	3,500
Pension contribution by Georgia	200
Income Tax	500
NIC (employee)	180
NIC (employer)	210
Trade union subscription	15

(a) Calculate the employer's pension contribution

£ _____

(b) Calculate Georgia's net salary for August

£ _____

(c) Transfer the pension liability from the salary control account to the pension liability account, using the picklist below.

Details		Debit £	Credit £
	▼		
	▼		

Picklist

Pension administrator
Salary control

(d) Complete the journal for the trade union subscription deduction

Details		Debit £	Credit
	▼		
	▼		

Picklist

Trade union subscription
Salary control

(e) Complete the journal for the payment of the net salary to Georgia on the 28th

Details		Debit £	Credit
	▼		
	▼		

Picklist

Bank
Salary control

(f) What is the total monthly cost to the company of employing Georgia?

£

Chapter 6 Errors and the trial balance

Task 6.1

You have the following information for your business, First Fashions:

(a) £50 has been debited to the discounts received account instead of the discounts allowed account.

(b) A payment of £200 for office expenses has been credited to the loan account instead of the bank current account.

(c) A credit customer, Kit & Company, has ceased trading, owing First Fashions £2,800 plus VAT. The net amount and VAT must be written off in the general ledger.

Record the journal entries needed in the general ledger to deal with this information.

Journals

(a)

Account names		Amount £	Debit ✓	Credit ✓
	▼			
	▼			

(b)

Account names		Amount £	Debit ✓	Credit ✓
	▼			
	▼			

(c)

Account names		Amount £	Debit ✓	Credit ✓
	▼			
	▼			
	▼			

Picklist

Bank current account
Discounts allowed
Discounts received
Irrecoverable debt expense
Loan account
Sales ledger control
VAT control

Task 6.2

A business extracts a trial balance in which the debit column totals £452,409 and the credit column totals £463,490.

What will be the balance on the suspense account? Tick whether this balance will be a debit or a credit.

Account name	Amount £	Debit ✓	Credit ✓
Suspense			

....

Task 6.3

A business used a suspense account with a credit balance of £124 to balance its initial trial balance.

Correction of which ONE of the following errors will clear the suspense account?

Error	✓
A credit note from a supplier with a net amount of £124 was not entered in the purchases ledger	
Discounts allowed of £124 were only posted to the discounts allowed account	
A cash purchase for £124 was not entered in the purchases account	
An irrecoverable debt write-off of £124 was not entered in the subsidiary ledger	

....

Task 6.4

Given below are two ledger accounts.

Examine them carefully and then using the picklist below to select the account, re-write them correcting any errors that have been made (you may assume that the balance brought forward on the VAT account is correct).

Sales ledger control

Details	Amount £	Details	Amount £
Sales	15,899	Balance b/f	1,683
Discounts allowed	900	Bank	14,228
Sales returns	1,467	Irrecoverable debt expense	245
		Balance c/d	2,110
	18,266		18,266

VAT control

Details	Amount £	Details	Amount £
Sales	2,368	Balance b/f	2,576
Purchase returns	115	Purchases	1,985
Balance c/d	2,078		
	4,561		4,561

Corrected accounts

Sales ledger control

Details	Amount £	Details	Amount £
▼		▼	
▼		▼	
		▼	
		▼	
		▼	

VAT control

Details	Amount £	Details	Amount £
▼		▼	
		▼	
▼		▼	

Picklist

Balance b/f
Balance c/d
Bank
Discounts allowed
Irrecoverable debt expense
Purchase returns
Purchases
Sales
Sales returns

Task 6.5

The trial balance of Harry Parker & Co has been prepared by the bookkeeper and the total of the debit balances is £427,365 while the total of the credit balances is £431,737. The difference was dealt with by setting up a suspense account and then the ledger accounts were investigated to try to find the causes of the difference. The following errors and omissions were found.

You are required to:

Draft journal entries to correct each of these errors or omissions.

(a) **The total of the sales day book was undercast by £1,000.**

Details		Debit £	Credit £
	▼		
	▼		

Picklist

Sales ledger control
Suspense

(b) **The balance on the electricity account of £1,642 had been completely omitted from the trial balance.**

Details		Debit £	Credit £
	▼		
	▼		

Picklist

Electricity
Suspense

(c) **Discounts allowed of £865 had been entered on the wrong side of the discounts allowed account.**

Details		Debit £	Credit £
	▼		
	▼		
	▼		
	▼		

Picklist

Discounts allowed
Suspense

(d) **Using the picklist below, write up the suspense account showing clearly the opening balance and how the suspense account is cleared after correction of each of the errors.**

Details		£	Details		£
	▼			▼	
				▼	
				▼	
				▼	

Picklist

Balance b/f
Discounts allowed
Electricity
Sales ledger control

Task 6.6

After extracting an initial trial balance a business finds it has a debit balance of £118 in the suspense account. A number of errors have been noted.

Using the picklists below, record the journal entries needed in the general ledger to reverse the incorrect entries and record the transactions correctly.

(a) **Sales of £500 have been credited to the sales returns account.**

Details		Debit £	Credit £
▼			
▼			

Picklist

Sales returns
Sales

(b) **Entries to record a bank payment of £125 for office expenses have been reversed.**

Details		Debit £	Credit £
▼			
▼			
▼			
▼			

Picklist

Bank
Office expenses

(c) **A bank payment of £299 for purchases (no VAT) has been entered correctly in the purchases column of the cash book but as £29 in the total column.**

Details		Debit £	Credit £
▼			
▼			
▼			
▼			
▼			

Picklist

Bank
Purchases
Suspense

(d) Discounts allowed of £388 were only posted to the sales ledger control account in the general ledger.

Details		Debit £	Credit £
	▼		
	▼		
	▼		
	▼		

Picklist

Discounts allowed
Sales ledger control
Suspense

Task 6.7

On 30 June, a suspense account of a business that is not registered for VAT has a credit balance of £720.

On 1 July, the following errors were discovered:

(i)   A bank payment of £225 has been omitted from the rent and rates account.

(ii) An irrecoverable debt expense of £945 has been credited correctly to the sales ledger control account, but debited to both the irrecoverable debt account and the sales account.

(a) Enter the opening balance in the suspense account below.

(b) Make the necessary entries to clear the suspense account using the picklist below.

Suspense

Date	Details	Amount £	Date	Details	Amount £
		▼			▼
		▼			▼

Picklist

Balance b/f
Bank
Sales

Task 6.8

(a) When posting an invoice received for building maintenance, £980 was entered on the building maintenance expense account instead of the correct amount of £890. In each case, select the correct option from the table below.

What correction should be made to the building maintenance expenses account?

	✓
Debit £90	
Credit £90	
Debit £1,780	
Credit £1,780	

(b) A business receives an invoice from a supplier for £2,800 which is mislaid before any entry has been made, resulting in the transaction being omitted from the books entirely.

This is an

	✓
Error of transposition	
Error of omission	
Error of principle	
Error of commission	

(c) **An error of commission is one where**

	✓
A transaction has not been recorded	
One side of a transaction has been recorded in the wrong account, and that account is of a different class to the correct account	
One side of a transaction has been recorded in the wrong account, and that account is of the same class as the correct account	
A transaction has been recorded using the wrong amount	

(d) **Which ONE of the following is an error of principle?**

	✓
A gas bill credited to the gas account and debited to the bank account	
The purchase of a non-current asset credited to the asset account and debited to the supplier's account	
The purchase of a non-current asset debited to the purchases account and credited to the supplier's account	
The payment of wages debited and credited to the correct accounts, but using the wrong amount	

Task 6.9

(a) **Where a transaction is entered into the correct ledger accounts, but the wrong amount is used, the error is known as an error of**

	✓
Omission	
Original entry	
Commission	
Principle	

(b) When a trial balance was prepared, two ledger accounts were omitted:

Discounts received   £6,150
Discounts allowed   £7,500

A suspense account was opened.

What was the balance on the suspense account?

	✓
Debit £1,350	
Credit £1,350	
Debit £13,650	
Credit £13,650	

(c) If a purchases return of £48 has been wrongly posted to the debit of the sales returns account, but has been correctly entered in the purchases ledger control account, the total of the trial balance would show

	✓
The credit side to be £48 more than the debit side	
The debit side to be £48 more than the credit side	
The credit side to be £96 more than the debit side	
The debit side to be £96 more than the credit side	

(d) Indicate whether preparing a trial balance will reveal the following errors.

	Yes	No
Omitting both entries for a transaction		
Posting the debit entry for an invoice to an incorrect expense account		
Omitting the debit entry for a transaction		
Posting the debit entry for a transaction as a credit entry		

Task 6.10

Show which of the errors below are, or are not, disclosed by the trial balance.

Error in the general ledger	Error disclosed by the trial balance ✓	Error NOT disclosed by the trial balance ✓
Recording a bank receipt of a cash sale on the debit side of the cash sales account		
Entering an insurance expense in the administration expenses account		
Entering the discounts received account balance on the debit side of the trial balance		
Miscasting the total column of one page of the sales returns day book		
Failing to write up a dishonoured cheque in the cash book		
Recording discount allowed of £15 as £150 in the cash book		

Task 6.11

Your organisation's trial balance included a suspense account. All the bookkeeping errors have now been traced and the journal entries shown below have been recorded.

Journal entries

Account name	Debit £	Credit £
Motor vehicles	4,300	
Machinery		4,300
Suspense	750	
Sales ledger control		750
Discounts allowed	209	
Suspense		209

Post the journal entries to the general ledger accounts Dates are not required but you must complete the 'details' columns accurately.

Discounts allowed

Details	Amount £	Details	Amount £
▼		▼	

Machinery

Details	Amount £	Details	Amount £
▼		▼	

Motor vehicles

Details	Amount £	Details	Amount £
▼		▼	

Sales ledger control

Details	Amount £	Details	Amount £
▼		▼	

Suspense

Details	Amount £	Details	Amount £
		Balance b/f	541

Picklist

Discounts allowed
Machinery
Motor vehicles
Sales ledger control
Suspense

Task 6.12

Your business extracted an initial trial balance which did not balance, and a suspense account with a debit balance of £6,290 was opened. Journal entries were subsequently prepared to correct the errors that had been found, and clear the suspense account. The list of balances in the initial trial balance, and the journal entries to correct the errors, are shown below.

Journal entries

Account name	Debit £	Credit £
Sales ledger control account	2,875	
Suspense		2,875
Sales ledger control account	2,875	
Suspense		2,875

Account name	Debit £	Credit £
Heat and light		5,172
Suspense	5,172	
Heat and light	5,712	
Suspense		5,712

Taking into account the journal entries, which will clear the suspense account, redraft the trial balance by writing the figures in the debit or credit column.

	Balances extracted on 30 June £	Balances at 1 July	
		Debit £	Credit £
Machinery	82,885		
Computer equipment	41,640		
Insurance	17,520		
Bank (overdraft)	13,252		
Petty cash	240		
Sales ledger control	241,500		
Purchases ledger control	134,686		
VAT (owing to HM Revenue and Customs)	19,920		
Capital	44,826		
Sales	525,092		
Purchases	269,400		
Purchases returns	16,272		
Wages	61,680		
Maintenance expenses	3,283		
Stationery	8,049		
Rent and rates	3,466		
Heat and light	5,172		
Telephone	7,596		
Marketing expenses	5,327		
Totals			

Task 6.13

Kitchen Kuts' initial trial balance includes a suspense account with a balance of £100.

The error has been traced to the sales returns day book shown below.

Sales returns day book

Date 20XX	Details	Credit note number	Total £	VAT £	Net £
30 June	Barber Bates Ltd	367	720	120	600
30 June	GTK Ltd	368	4,320	720	3,600
30 June	Peer Prints	369	960	160	800
	Totals		6,000	1,100	5,000

(a) Identify the error and record the journal entries needed in the general ledger to

    (i) Remove the incorrect entry

Account name	Amount £	Debit ✓	Credit ✓
▼			

    (ii) Record the correct entry

Account name	Amount £	Debit ✓	Credit ✓
▼			

    (iii) Remove the suspense account balance

Account name	Amount £	Debit ✓	Credit ✓
▼			

An entry to record a bank payment of £350 for heat and light has been reversed.

(b) Record the journal entries needed in the general ledger to

    (i) Remove the incorrect entries

Account name	Amount £	Debit ✓	Credit ✓
▼			
▼			

(ii) Record the correct entries

Account name	Amount £	Debit ✓	Credit ✓
▼			
▼			

Picklist

Bank
Heat and light
Suspense
VAT

Answer bank

Answer bank

Bookkeeping Controls Answer bank

Chapter 1

Task 1.1

	Comments
Cheque from B B Berry Ltd	Amount: Words and figures differ, they should match to verify the correct amount payable.
Cheque from Q Q Stores	Signature: Cheque is unsigned. Cheques must be signed by an authorised signatory.
Cheque from Dagwell Enterprises	Payee: Payee name is incorrect – Electronics instead of Electrical
Cheque from Weller Enterprises	Date: Dated 6 January 20X5 instead of 20X6 – this cheque is therefore out of date. Although cheques have no expiry date, generally accepted banking convention is that cheques are not accepted after 6 months. This is due to the possibility of duplication of payment or this being a stolen cheque.

Task 1.2

	Payment method	Comment
Payment to Kim Guitars Ltd for £2500 for items purchased on credit. The payment is required within 5 days	BACS direct credit	No urgency on the payment, so BACS is sufficient
Payment of £1000 to Pixie Bass as a deposit on a supply. The payment is required today to release the shipment	Faster payment	Same day money transfer is required.
Payment of £265,000 to Paz Ltd to secure a new retail unit. Immediate payment is required	CHAPS	A highly secure way of moving large amounts of money
Payment to Santiago Strings for £875 to pay an invoice due by the end of the week	BACS direct credit	No urgency on the payment, so BACS direct credit is sufficient

Task 1.3

(a) A $\boxed{\text{standing order}}$ would be set up to repay a bank loan in equal monthly instalments.

(b) A $\boxed{\text{direct debit}}$ would be set up to make the minimum payment on a credit card by variable amounts each month.

(c) A bank $\boxed{\text{overdraft}}$ would be arranged when short-term borrowing is needed.

Task 1.4

Situation	Solution
Making regular rent payments	Standing order
Purchase of office stationery online	Debit card
Payment of wages to staff	BACS direct credit
Payment of £2500 to a supplier after taking 15 days credit	BACS direct credit
Buying tea bags for the office	Cash
Payment of £375 for new tyres for the company van.	Debit card

A standing order will ensure that regular, same value payments are made on the same day every month to ensure the rent is paid on time without fail.

Buying office stationery online requires payment by a debit (or credit card)

Payment of wages by BACS Direct Credit ensures that the money is securely sent to the correct recipient. It also reduces the amount of cash which is kept on the business premises.

Payments to supplier after receipt of an invoice are made by BACS. This ensures the correct amount is sent directly to the correct recipient, within the credit terms set. Payment may also be made by cheque, but this is not an option in this scenario.

Teabags and small items for the office are usually purchased using petty cash, due to the small payments required.

The tyres would have required immediate payment at the garage, so the debit card would be the most suitable form of payment as it securely ensures immediate payment.

Task 1.5

	✓
Funds are available in customer's account	
Issue number	
Words and figures match	✓
Security number	
Expiry date	
Date is not in the future	✓

Task 1.6

The director of Parker Flooring Limited has made a number of payments today (2 February 20X6) in respect of materials for the company. Select the correct impact on the bank account

Payment	Impact on the bank account	Comment
Cheque written for £550 to Soft Carpets Limited	Delayed	The money leaves Parker Flooring's account when the cheque is presented at the bank which may be several days after the cheque was issued
Debit card to buy diesel for the van £65	Immediate	Usually reflected in the bank account within a few hours as the debit card draws money from the account
Credit card to buy printer cartridges online £30	Delayed	This will be charged to the credit card account, and the only impact on the bank will be once the monthly payment to the credit card company is made, therefore a delayed impact
Payment of a purchase invoice using BACS Direct Credit to Solvit Limited £1200	Immediate	Parker Flooring will see the cash leave their account immediately, although it may take up to three days to be shown in the supplier account. It depends on the banks
Cheque written for £276 to Wall2Wall Limited	Delayed	The money leaves Parker Flooring's account when the cheque is presented at the bank which may be several days

BPP
LEARNING MEDIA

Payment	Impact on the bank account	Comment
Debit card to buy coffee from the local store of £5.67	Immediate	Usually reflected in the bank account within a few hours as the debit card draws money from the account
Bank draft for £10,000 to purchase a new van	Immediate	Although the bank draft cheque is drawn on the bank's current account, the bank will immediately withdraw the funds from Parker Flooring's account once they authorise the draft

Task 1.7

Who is the drawee?	First National
Who is the payee?	J Peterson
Who is the drawer?	F Ronald

Chapter 2

Task 2.1

Transaction	Payment out ✓	Payment in ✓
£470.47 paid into the bank		✓
Standing order of £26.79	✓	
Cheque payment of £157.48	✓	
Interest earned on the bank balance		✓
BACS payment for wages	✓	

Task 2.2

(a)

Date	Details	Bank £
	Bal b/f	379.22
27 Jan	Tunfield DC	594.69
27 Jan	Tunshire CO	468.29
27 Jan	Non-credit sales	478.90
27 Jan	Tunfield BB	1,059.72
27 Jan	Non-credit sales	752.16
27 Jan	Non-credit sales	256.80
		3,989.78

Answer bank

(b)

Unmatched item		Action to be taken	Explanation
Bank credit	108.51	Update cash book	This must be checked to any supporting documentation such as any remittance advice from Tunfield AOS or the original invoice – when it has been checked the amount should be entered into the cash book
Standing order British Elec	212.00	Update cash book	The standing order schedule should be checked to ensure that this is correct and it should then be entered into the cash book
Bank interest received	3.68	Update cash book	This should be entered into the cash book
Sales of CDs	256.80	Include on bank reconciliation	The £256.80 cash sales of CDs settled by cheque do not appear on the bank statement. This is an outstanding lodgement that will appear in the bank reconciliation statement
Cheque number 003016	144.67	Include on bank reconciliation	Unpresented cheque – will appear in the bank reconciliation statement
Cheque number 003018	44.79	Include on bank reconciliation	Unpresented cheque – will appear in the bank reconciliation statement
Cheque number 003019	273.48	Include on bank reconciliation	Unpresented cheque – will appear in the bank reconciliation statement

(c) **Cash book**

Date	Details	Bank £	Cheque number	Details	Bank £
	Balance b/f	379.22	003014	Henson Press	329.00
27 Jan	Tunfield DC	594.69	003015	Ely Instr	736.96
27 Jan	Tunshire CO	468.29	003016	Jester Press	144.67
27 Jan	Non-credit sales	478.90	003017	CD Supplies	74.54
27 Jan	Tunfield BB	1,059.72	003018	Jester Press	44.79
27 Jan	Non-credit sales	752.16	003019	Buser Ltd	273.48
27 Jan	Non-credit sales	256.80	SO	Rates	255.00
27 Jan	Bank interest	3.68	DD	Rent	500.00
27 Jan	Tunfield AOS	108.51	SO	Standing order British Elec	212.00
				Balance c/d	1,531.53
	Total	4,101.97		Total	4,101.97

(d)

Bank reconciliation statement	£
Balance as per bank statement	1,737.67
Add:	
Non-credit sales	256.80
Total to add	256.80
Less:	
Cheque 003016	144.67
Cheque 003018	44.79
Cheque 003019	273.48
Total to subtract	462.94
Balance as per cash book	1,531.53

Task 2.3

Cash book

Date	Details	Bank £	Date	Cheque no.	Details	Bank £
01 Nov	Balance b/f	5,466	03 Nov	110870	Roberts & Co	6,250
24 Nov	Bevan & Co	1,822	03 Nov	110871	J Jones	1,164
24 Nov	Plant Pots Ltd	7,998	06 Nov	110872	Lake Walks Ltd	2,250
21 Nov	BBT Ltd	10,000	10 Nov	110873	PH Supplies	275
24 Nov	Petals Ltd	2,555	17 Nov	110874	Peters & Co	76
			21 Nov	DD	Insurance Ensured	500
			24 Nov	DD	Rainbow Ltd	88
			28 Nov		Balance c/d	17,238
	Total	27,841			Total	27,841
29 Nov	Balance b/d	17,238				

Note. Cheque number 110865 on the bank statement: the first cheque in the cash book in November is number 110870. As the difference between the opening balances on the bank statement and in the cash book is for the amount of this cheque (£3,670) it is reasonable to assume that cheque 110865 was entered in the cash book in a previous month and would have been a reconciling item in the bank reconciliation in the previous month. This cheque should be ticked to the October bank reconciliation.

Bank reconciliation statement as at 28 November	£
Balance as per bank statement	7,769
Add:	
Bevan & Co	1,822
Plant Pots Ltd	7,998
Total to add	9,820
Less:	
PH Supplies	275
Peters & Co	76
Total to subtract	351
Balance as per cash book	17,238

Task 2.4

(a)

	Timing difference? ✓
Bank charges not recorded in the cash book	
Outstanding lodgements	✓
Interest charged not recorded in the cash book	
Unpresented cheques	✓

(b)

	✓
£714 overdrawn	
£657 overdrawn	✓
£473 overdrawn	
£530 overdrawn	

Working:

£(565) o/d - £92 dishonoured cheque = £(657) o/d.

The £57 will not yet have affected the bank account as not been presented at bank yet, hence it does not affect the bank balance as at 31 December.

(c)

	✓
£5,100 overdrawn	
£6,000 overdrawn	
£6,250 overdrawn	
£6,450 overdrawn	✓

Workings:

	£	£
Balance b/f		5,675
Reversal – Standing order entered twice	125	
Reversal – Dishonoured cheque entered in error as a debit		450
Correction – Dishonoured cheque		450
Balance c/d (overdraft)	6,450	
	6,575	6,575

Task 2.5

(a)

	✓
£1,460	
£2,300	✓
£2,580	
£3,140	

Workings:

	£
Cash book balance	2,490
Adjustment re charges	(50)
Adjustment re dishonoured cheque from customer	(140)
	2,300

(b)

	✓
Receipts of £250 recorded in the cash book, but not yet recorded by bank	
Bank charges of £250 shown on the bank statement, not in the cash book	
Standing orders of £250 included on bank statement, not in the cash book	
Cheques issued for £250 recorded in the cash book, but not yet gone through the bank account	✓

All the other options would give the bank account £250 less than the cash book.

(c) The correct answer is:

£	3,366

Workings:

	£
Balance per cash book	3,526
Plus: bank interest received	150
Less: dishonoured cheque	(310)
Amended cash book balance	3,366

....

Task 2.6

Cash book

Date	Details	Bank £	Date	Cheque number	Details	Bank £
01 Jul	Balance b/f	1,855	01 Jul	126459	Gumpley Co	3,283
20 Jul	Brimfull Ltd	5,483	01 Jul	126460	Warnes Ltd	1,209
21 Jul	Adera Ltd	2,198	01 Jul	126461	Veldt Partners	4,221
22 Jul	Mist Northern	1,004	01 Jul	126462	Pathways	1,117
9 Jul	Snip Snap Co	8,845	02 Jul	126463	Lindstrom Co	846
			02 Jul	126464	Kestrels Training	658
			13 Jul	126465	HGW Ltd	3,200
			13 Jul		Flit DC	500
			18 Jul		Consol Landlords	475
			20 Jul		Bank charges	32
			22 Jul		Interest	103
			23 Jul		Balance c/d	3,741
	Total	19,385			Total	19,385
24 Jul	Balance b/d	3,741				

Bank reconciliation statement as at 23 July	£
Balance per bank statement	4,585
Add:	
Adera Ltd	2,198
Mist Northern	1,004
Total to add	3,202
Less:	
Lindstrom Co	846
HGW Ltd	3,200
Total to subtract	4,046
Balance as per cash book	3,741

Chapter 3

Task 3.1

(a)

Account	Amount £	Debit	Credit
Purchase ledger control	3,390		3,390
VAT control	565	565	
Purchases	2,825	2,825	

(b)

Account	Amount £	Debit	Credit
Sales ledger control	1,860		1,860
VAT control	310	310	
Sales returns	1,550	1,550	

(c)

Account	Amount £	Debit	Credit
Bank	4,590		4,590
Purchase ledger control	4,590	4,590	

(d)

Account	Amount £	Debit	Credit
Bank	5,480	5,480	
Sales ledger control	5,480		5,480

Task 3.2

Sales ledger control

	£		£
Balance b/f	11,689	Sales returns	1,582
Sales	12,758	Bank	11,563
		Discounts allowed	738
		Balance c/d	10,564
	24,447		24,447

Task 3.3

Purchases ledger control

	£		£
Purchases returns	728	Balance b/f	8,347
Bank	8,837	Purchases	9,203
Discounts received	382		
Balance c/d	7,603		
	17,550		17,550

Task 3.4

Purchases ledger control

Date	Details	Amount £	Date	Details	Amount £
30 June	Bank	33,106	1 June	Balance b/f	85,299
30 June	Discounts received	1,000	30 June	Purchases	39,300
30 June	Purchases returns	275			
30 June	Balance c/d	90,218			
		124,599			124,599
			1 July	Balance b/d	90,218

Task 3.5

(a)

	✓
£32,125	✓
£33,975	
£34,725	
£33,225	

Working: £

Brought forward balance   31,475 (existing outstanding debt)
Sales   125,000
Less payments   (122,500)
Less credit notes   (1,300)
Less discounts   (550)
                                                   ‾‾‾‾‾‾
Total   32,125
                                                   ‾‾‾‾‾‾

(b)

	✓
£38,100	✓
£40,500	
£47,500	
£49,900	

Working:
                                                   £
Opening balance   34,500
Credit purchases   78,400
Discounts received   (1,200)
Payments   (68,900)
Purchases returns   (4,700)
                                                   ‾‾‾‾‾‾
                                                   38,100
                                                   ‾‾‾‾‾‾

Task 3.6

(a)

Details	Amount £	Details	Amount £
VAT on purchases	2,500	Balance b/f	4,500
VAT on sales returns	300	VAT on sales	6,000
Payment to HMRC	7,000	VAT on purchase returns	250
Balance c/d	950		
	10,750		10,750
		Balance b/d	950

(b)   The answer is

£	5,450

Balance b/d at 31 March 20XX of £950 plus the VAT of £4,500 on sales made during April

Chapter 4

Task 4.1

	Control account ✓	List of balances ✓	Both ✓
Invoice entered into the sales day book as £980 instead of £890			✓
Purchases day book overcast by £1,000	✓		
Discounts allowed of £20 not entered into the cash book (debit side)			✓
An invoice taken as £340 instead of £440 when being posted to the customer's account		✓	
Incorrect balancing of a memorandum ledger account		✓	
A purchases return not entered into the purchases returns day book			✓

··

Task 4.2

Sales ledger control

Details	Amount £	Details	Amount £
Balance b/f	5,000	Bank (2,400 + 3,600 +1,100 + 4,800)	11,900
Sales (2,000 + 2,700 + 1,100 + 3,800)	9,600	Balance c/d	2,700
	14,600		14,600
Balance b/d	2,700		

Sales ledger

H Simms

Details	Amount £	Details	Amount £
Balance b/f	900	Bank	2,400
Sales	2,000	Balance c/d	500
	2,900		2,900
Balance b/d	500		

P Good

Details	Amount £	Details	Amount £
Balance b/f	1,600	Bank	3,600
Sales	2,700	Balance c/d	700
	4,300		4,300
Balance b/d	700		

K Mitchell

Details	Amount £	Details	Amount £
Sales	1,100	Bank	1,100

C Brown

Details	Amount £	Details	Amount £
Balance b/f	2,500	Bank	4,800
Sales	3,800	Balance c/d	1,500
	6,300		6,300
Balance b/d	1,500		

Reconciliation of sales ledger balances with control account balance

	£
H Simms	500
P Good	700
K Mitchell	-
C Brown	1,500
Sales ledger control account	2,700

....

Task 4.3

Purchases ledger control

Details	Amount £	Details	Amount £
Bank		Balance b/f	2,700
(1,700 + 3,200 + 3,000)	7,900	Purchases	
Balance c/d	2,100	(1,600 + 2,500 + 3,200)	7,300
	10,000		10,000
		Balance b/d	2,100

Purchases ledger

J Peters

Details	Amount £	Details	Amount £
Bank	1,700	Balance b/f	300
Balance c/d	200	Purchases	1,600
	1,900		1,900
		Balance b/d	200

T Sands

Details	Amount £	Details	Amount £
Bank	3,200	Balance b/f	1,700
Balance c/d	1,000	Purchases	2,500
	4,200		4,200
		Balance b/d	1,000

L Farmer

Details	Amount £	Details	Amount £
Bank	3,000	Balance b/f	700
Balance c/d	900	Purchases	3,200
	3,900		3,900
		Balance b/d	900

Reconciliation of purchases ledger balances with control account balance

	£
J Peters	200
T Sands	1,000
L Farmer	900
Purchases ledger control account	2,100

Task 4.4

Sales ledger control

Details	Amount £	Details	Amount £
Balance b/f	9,450	Returns	700
Sales on credit	14,500	Bank	15,600
		Balance c/d	7,650
	23,950		23,950
Balance b/d	7,650		

(b) £90 which is the difference between the sales ledger control account balance of £7,650 (balance b/d) and the total balances on the sales ledger (3,000+1,250+3,310 = £7.650)

(c)

Reasons		Explanation
A cash receipt was incorrectly entered onto the customer's account in the sales ledger	✓	As the sales ledger is lower than the sales ledger control account, it is possible that a cash receipt was incorrectly entered onto the customer account.
A sales invoice has been duplicated in the sales ledger	☐	This would increase the sales ledger, so that the sales ledger would be GREATER than the sales ledger control.
A sales return credit note has only been recorded in the sales ledger control account	☐	This would reduce the sales ledger control account, so that the sales ledger would be GREATER than the sales ledger control.
Discounts have been posted twice in the customer's sales ledger account	✓	As the sales ledger is lower than the sales ledger control account, it is possible that discounts have been duplicated on the customer account.

Task 4.5

(a)

Purchase ledger control

Details	Amount £	Details	Amount £
Bank	9,750	Balance b/d	12,500
Discounts received	500	Purchases	8,600
Balance c/d	10,850		
	21,100		21,100
		Balance b/d	10,850

(b)

	£
Purchase ledger control account balance as at 31 July 20XX	10,850
Total of the purchase ledger accounts as at 31 July 20XX	10,650
Difference	200

(c)

Reason		Explanation
Purchases on credit have been recorded on the debit side of the purchase ledger	✓	This would decrease the balance on the purchase ledger, therefore making it less than the control account balance.
A purchase invoice has been duplicated in the purchase ledger	☐	This would increase the balance on the purchase ledger
Discounts received have been omitted from the purchases ledger but recorded in the purchases ledger control account	☐	This makes the balance on the purchase ledger control account lower than that on the purchase ledger
A cash payment to a credit supplier has been booked to the purchase ledger control account only	☐	This makes the balance on the purchase ledger control account lower than that on the purchase ledger

Task 4.6

(a)

Sales ledger control

Date	Details	Amount £	Date	Details	Amount £
01 Nov	Balance b/f	48,125	30 Nov	Bank	28,327
30 Nov	Sales	37,008	30 Nov	Discounts allowed	240
			30 Nov	Sales returns	2,316
			30 Nov	Balance c/d	54,250
		85,133			85,133
01 Dec	Balance b/d	54,250			

(b)

	£
Sales ledger control account balance as at 1 December	54,250
Total of sales ledger accounts as at 1 December	54,163
Difference	87

(c)

	✓
VAT has been overstated on an invoice.	
VAT has been understated on an invoice.	
A sales invoice has been entered in the sales ledger twice.	
A sales credit note has been entered in the sales ledger twice.	✓
A receipt from a customer has been omitted from the sales ledger.	
A receipt from a customer has been entered in the sales ledger twice.	✓

Task 4.7

(a)

Transactions	Amount £	VAT £
Sales on credit including VAT at 20%	106,800	17,800
Purchases on credit including VAT at 20%	54,000	9,000
Credit notes issued including VAT at 20%	2,820	470

(b)

Details	Amount £	Details	Amount £
Sales returns	470	Sales	17,800
Purchases	9,000		
Balance c/d	8,330		
	17,800		17,800
		Balance b/d	8,330

(c) The answer is

£	8,330

Task 4.8

(a)

Reason	
The sales ledger control account shows a difference to the sales ledger account balances	
Sales were less than purchases for the quarter	✓
There was an underpayment of VAT in the previous quarter	

A difference on the sales ledger control account would have no impact on the VAT due, and an underpayment of VAT in the prior period would not result in a repayment from HMRC.

(b)   The correct answer is:

£	21,540

Working:

£129,240 × 20/120 = £21,540

....

Task 4.9

(a)

	✓
The supplier sent an invoice for £150 which you have not yet received	
The supplier has allowed you £150 settlement discount which you had not entered in your ledger	✓
You have paid the supplier £150 which he has not yet accounted for	
You have returned goods worth £150 which the supplier has not yet accounted for	

All other options would lead to a higher balance in the supplier's records.

(b)

	✓
The control account only	
The list of balances only	
Both the control account and the list of balances	✓

(c)

Amount £	Debit ✓	Credit ✓
46,167		✓

Working:

	£		£
Debit entries	24,500	Credit entries	76,961
SO Payment	1,606		
Correction (need to remove from PLCA)	4,688		
Balance c/d	46,167		
	76,961		76,961

Once the balance is brought down at the start of the next period, it appears in the credit column

---

Task 4.10

(a)

	✓
The balance on the bank statement	
The balance on the sales ledger control account	✓
The balance on the purchases ledger control account	
The total of all the purchases ledger balances	
The total of all the sales ledger balances	✓

(b)

	✓
How much is owed to suppliers at any point	
Over how many months the outstanding balance owed by each individual credit customer has built up	✓
The total purchases over the year to date to each credit supplier	

Task 4.11

Account name	Amount £	Debit ✓	Credit ✓
Irrecoverable debts	1,560	✓	
VAT control	312	✓	
Sales ledger control	1,872		✓

Details	Amount £	Details	Amount £
		Balance b/f	250
Purchases	90	Sales	1,400
Sales returns	50		
Irrecoverable debt expense	312		
Balance c/d	1,198		
	1,650		1,650
		Balance b/d	1,198

Task 4.12

Journal

Account name	Amount £	Debit ✓	Credit ✓
Irrecoverable debt expense	240	✓	
VAT control(£240 × 20% = £48)	48	✓	
Sales ledger control	288		✓

Task 4.13

Account name	Amount £	Debit ✓	Credit ✓
Irrecoverable debt expense	1,975	✓	
VAT control	395	✓	
Sales ledger control	2,370		✓

BPP
LEARNING MEDIA

Chapter 5

Task 5.1

Journal

Account name	Debit £	Credit £
Capital		10,000
Furniture and fittings	15,315	
Motor vehicles	20,109	
Cash at bank	15,000	
Purchases ledger control		37,238
Sales ledger control	12,524	
Loan from bank		7,000
VAT (owed to HM Revenue & Customs)		8,710
Totals	62,948	62,948

Task 5.2

Account name	Amount £	Debit ✓	Credit ✓
Petty cash control	200	✓	
Bank	300	✓	
Capital	500		✓
Van	6,000	✓	
Trade receivables	7,700	✓	
Loan from bank	9,000		✓
VAT control (owed to HM Revenue & Customs)	1,300		✓
Trade creditors	3,400		✓

Task 5.3

Account name	Amount £	Debit ✓	Credit ✓
Cash	150	✓	
Cash at bank	12,350	✓	
Capital	23,456		✓
Fixtures and fittings	2,100	✓	
Trade receivables	3,206	✓	
Loan from bank	10,000		✓
Motor vehicle	15,650	✓	

··

Task 5.4

(a) The correct answer is:

£	1,761

Working:

	£
Gross salary	2,200
Income tax	(256)
Employees' NIC	(183)
Net salary	1,761

(b)

Salary expense

	£		£
Salary control	2,200		
Salary control	200		

Salary control

	£		£
Bank	1,761	Salary expense	2,200
HMRC control	183	Salary expense	200
HMRC control	256		
HMRC control	200		

HMRC control

	£		£
		Salary control	200
		Salary control	256
		Salary control	183

Bank

	£		£
		Salary control	1,761

Task 5.5

Select the correct recipient of each of the following payroll related costs

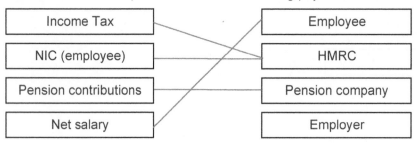

Income Tax		Employee
NIC (employee)		HMRC
Pension contributions		Pension company
Net salary		Employer

Task 5.6

(a)

£	140

Workings

£3,500 × 0.04

(b)

£	2,605

Workings

Net salary is £2,605 (3,500 – 200 – 500 – 180 – 15)

(c)   Journal

Details	Debit £	Credit £
Salary control (200+140)	340	
Pension administrator		340

(d)   Journal

Details	Debit £	Credit £
Salary control	15	
Trade union subscription		15

(e)   Journal

Details	Debit £	Credit £
Bank		2,605
Salary control	2,605	

(f)

£	3,850

Workings

Gross salary of £3,500 + Employer NIC of £210 + Pension contributions of 4% of gross salary of £140

Chapter 6

Task 6.1

Journals

(a)

Account names	Amount £	Debit ✓	Credit ✓
Discounts allowed	50	✓	
Discounts received	50		✓

(b)

Account names	Amount £	Debit ✓	Credit ✓
Loan account	200	✓	
Bank current account	200		✓

(c)

Account names	Amount £	Debit ✓	Credit ✓
Irrecoverable debt expense	2,800	✓	
VAT control	560	✓	
Sales ledger control	3,360		✓

Task 6.2

Account name	Amount £	Debit ✓	Credit ✓
Suspense	11,081	✓	

Task 6.3

Error	✓
A credit note from a supplier with a net amount of £124 was not entered in the purchases ledger	
Discounts allowed of £124 were only posted to the discounts allowed account	✓
A cash purchase for £124 was not entered in the purchases account	
An irrecoverable debt write-off of £124 was not entered in the subsidiary ledger	

Task 6.4

Sales ledger control

Details	Amount £	Details	Amount £
Balance b/f	1,683	Bank	14,228
Sales	15,899	Discounts allowed	900
		Irrecoverable debts expense	245
		Sales returns	1,467
		Balance c/d	742
	17,582		17,582

VAT control

Details	Amount £	Details	Amount £
Purchases	1,985	Balance b/f	2,576
		Sales	2,368
Balance c/d	3,074	Purchase returns	115
	5,059		5,059

Task 6.5

(a) Journal entries

Details	Debit £	Credit £
Sales ledger control	1,000	
Suspense		1,000

(b) Journal entries

Details	Debit £	Credit £
Electricity	1,642	
Suspense		1,642

(c) Journal entries

Details	Debit £	Credit £
Discounts allowed (to reverse the error)	865	
Suspense		865
Discounts allowed (to record the correct entry)	865	
Suspense		865

(d) Suspense account

Details	£	Details	£
Balance b/f	4,372	Sales ledger control	1,000
		Electricity	1,642
		Discounts allowed	865
		Discounts allowed	865
	4,372		4,372

Task 6.6

The journals

(a)

Details	Debit £	Credit £
Sales returns	500	
Sales		500

(b)

Details	Debit £	Credit £
Office expenses	125	
Bank		125
Office expenses	125	
Bank		125

(c)

Details	Debit £	Credit £
Bank	29	
Suspense	270	
Purchases		299
Purchases	299	
Bank		299

(d)

Details	Debit £	Credit £
Sales ledger control	388	
Suspense		388
Discounts allowed	388	
Sales ledger control		388

Task 6.7

Suspense

Date	Details	Amount £	Date	Details	Amount £
01 July	Sales	945	30 June	Balance b/f	720
			01 July	Bank (rent & rates)	225
		945			945

Task 6.8

(a)

	✓
Debit £90	
Credit £90	✓
Debit £1,780	
Credit £1,780	

£890 should have been debited to the expense account. Instead, £980 has been debited. To bring this amount down to £890, the expense account should be credited with £90.

(b)

	✓
Error of transposition	
Error of omission	✓
Error of principle	
Error of commission	

(c)

	✓
A transaction has not been recorded	
One side of a transaction has been recorded in the wrong account, and that account is of a different class to the correct account	
One side of a transaction has been recorded in the wrong account, and that account is of the same class as the correct account	✓
A transaction has been recorded using the wrong amount	

(d)

	✓
A gas bill credited to the gas account and debited to the bank account	
The purchase of a non-current asset credited to the asset account and debited to the supplier's account	
The purchase of a non-current asset debited to the purchases account and credited to the supplier's account	✓
The payment of wages debited and credited to the correct accounts, but using the wrong amount	

....

Task 6.9

(a)

	✓
Omission	
Original entry	✓
Commission	
Principle	

(b)

	✓
Debit £1,350	✓
Credit £1,350	
Debit £13,650	
Credit £13,650	

Workings:

Suspense account

Details	Amount £	Details	Amount £
Opening balance	1,350	Discounts allowed	7,500
Discounts received	6,150		
	7,500		7,500

(c) The correct answer is: The debit side to be £96 more than the credit side

Working:

Debits will exceed credits by 2 × £48 = £96

(d)

	Yes	No
Omitting both entries for a transaction		✓
Posting the debit entry for an invoice to an incorrect expense account		✓
Omitting the debit entry for a transaction	✓	
Posting the debit entry for a transaction as a credit entry	✓	

Task 6.10

Error in the general ledger	Error disclosed by the trial balance ✓	Error NOT disclosed by the trial balance ✓
Recording a bank receipt of a cash sale on the debit side of the cash sales account	✓	
Entering an insurance expense in the administration expenses account		✓
Entering the discounts received account balance on the debit side of the trial balance	✓	
Miscasting the total column of one page of the sales returns day book	✓	
Failing to write up a dishonoured cheque in the cash book		✓
Recording discount allowed of £15 as £150 in the cash book		✓

....

Task 6.11

Discounts allowed

Details	Amount £	Details	Amount £
Suspense	209		

Machinery

Details	Amount £	Details	Amount £
		Motor vehicles	4,300

Motor vehicles

Details	Amount £	Details	Amount £
Machinery	4,300		

Sales ledger control

Details	Amount £	Details	Amount £
		Suspense	750

Suspense

Details	Amount £	Details	Amount £
Sales ledger control	750	Balance b/f	541
		Discounts allowed	209

Task 6.12

Workings to the answer (for information only)

Suspense

Details	Amount £	Details	Amount £
Balance b/f	6,290	Sales ledger control	2,875
Heat and light	5,172	Sales ledger control	2,875
		Heat and light	5,712
	11,462		11,462

Heat & Light

Details	Amount £	Details	Amount £
Balance b/f	5,172	Suspense	5,172
Suspense	5,712	Balance c/d	5,712

Sales ledger control

Details	Amount £	Details	Amount £
Balance b/f	241,500		
Suspense	2,875		
Suspense	2,875	Balance c/d	247,250
	247,250		247,250

Answer

	Balances extracted on 30 June £	Balances at 1 July Debit £	Balances at 1 July Credit £
Machinery	82,885	82,885	
Computer equipment	41,640	41,640	
Insurance	17,520	17,520	
Bank (overdraft)	13,252		13,252
Petty cash	240	240	
Sales ledger control	241,500	247,250	
Purchases ledger control	134,686		134,686
VAT (owing to HM Revenue and Customs)	19,920		19,920
Capital	44,826		44,826
Sales	525,092		525,092
Purchases	269,400	269,400	
Purchases returns	16,272		16,272
Wages	61,680	61,680	
Maintenance expenses	3,283	3,283	
Stationery	8,049	8,049	
Rent and rates	3,466	3,466	
Heat and light	5,172	5,712	
Telephone	7,596	7,596	
Marketing expenses	5,327	5,327	
Totals		754,048	754,048

Task 6.13

(a)

(i)

Account name	Amount £	Debit ✓	Credit ✓
VAT	1,100		✓

(ii)

Account name	Amount £	Debit ✓	Credit ✓
VAT	1,000	✓	

(iii)

Account name	Amount £	Debit ✓	Credit ✓
Suspense	100	✓	

(b)

(i)

Account name	Amount £	Debit ✓	Credit ✓
Heat and light	350	✓	
Bank	350		✓

(ii)

Account name	Amount £	Debit ✓	Credit ✓
Heat and light	350	✓	
Bank	350		✓

AAT AQ2016 SAMPLE ASSESSMENT
Bookkeeping Controls

Time allowed: 2 hours

Bookkeeping Controls
AAT sample assessment

Task 1 (12 marks)

Organisations use different payment methods.

(a) **Match each situation with the most appropriate payment method below, payment methods may be used more than once.**

(CBT instructions: Click on a box in the left column then on one in the right column to indicate each answer. To remove a line, click on it.)

Situation	Payment method
Making a payment via the internet to purchase office stationery	Standing order
	Cheque
Making a non-automated low value payment in person	Bank draft
	Debit card
Making a payment by post to a credit supplier	CHAPS
Making regular payments of regular amounts to the same recipient	Cash

(b) **Show which TWO of the payment methods below will not reduce funds in the payer's bank balance on the date of payment by writing the relevant payment methods from the drop-down list below.**

Payment method
▼
▼

Picklist

CHAPS
Cheque
Credit card
Direct debit
Standing order

It is important to understand the effect of errors in a bookkeeping system.

(c) **Show whether the errors below will cause an imbalance in the trial balance by writing the appropriate answer against each error. You may use each answer more than once.**

Error	Effect on trial balance
A cash sale has been recorded in the sales and VAT control accounts only.	▼
The purchase of a new computer has been recorded in the office expenses account. All other entries were correct.	▼
A BACS payment to a credit supplier was debited to the bank account and credited to the purchases ledger control account.	▼
A cash payment of £56 for stationery has been recorded in the cash account as £65. All other entries were correct.	▼

Picklist

Will cause an imbalance
Will not cause an imbalance

(d) **Show which ONE of the errors below is an error of principle.**

Error	
A cash sale has been recorded in the sales and VAT control accounts only.	☐
The purchase of a new computer has been recorded in the office expenses account. All other entries were correct.	☐
A BACS payment to a credit supplier was debited to the bank account and credited to the purchases ledger control account.	☐
A cash payment of £56 for stationery has been recorded in the cash account as £65. All other entries were correct.	☐

The correction of errors in a bookkeeping system is recorded in the journal.

(e) **Which other transaction from the drop-down list below would be recorded in the journal.**

| ▼ |

Picklist

Interest received from the bank
Irrecoverable debts written off
Prompt payment discounts received
Re-imbursement of petty cash

Task 2 (12 marks)

Payroll transactions are recorded using a wages control account.

This is a note from your line manager.

The wages expense for June is £70,560. Other payroll information for the month is shown below.

Income tax and National Insurance amounts are as follows:

* Income tax: £7,125
* Employer's NI: £5,222
* Employees' NI: £4,657

In addition there are voluntary deductions for 42 employees who each pay £15 a month for trade union fees.

Show the journal entries needed to record:

* **The net wages paid to employees**
* **The HM Revenue and Customs liability**
* **The trade union liability**

Journal to record the net wages paid to employees

Account name		Debit £	Credit £
	▼		
	▼		

Picklist

Bank
Employee's NI
Employer's NI
HM Revenue and Customs
Income tax
Trade union
Wages control
Wages expense

Journal to record the HM Revenue and Customs liability

Account name		Debit £	Credit £
	▼		
	▼		

Picklist

Bank
Employee's NI
Employer's NI
HM Revenue and Customs
Income tax
Trade union
Wages control
Wages expense

Journal to record the trade union liability

Account name		Debit £	Credit £
	▼		
	▼		

Picklist

Bank
Employee's NI
Employer's NI
HM Revenue and Customs
Income tax
Trade union
Wages control
Wages expense

....

Task 3 (10 marks)

This is a customer's account in the sales ledger.

Zoe Daniels

Date 20XX	Details	Amount £	Date 20XX	Details	Amount £
01 Jun	Balance b/f	984	3 Jun	Credit note 98	317
10 Jun	Invoice 812	1,248	15 Jun	Credit note 103	163

The customer has now ceased trading owing the amount outstanding, which includes VAT.

(a) **Record the journal entries needed in the general ledger to write off the net amount and the VAT. Do not enter a zero in unused debit or credit column cells.**

Journal

Account name		Debit £	Credit £
	▾		
	▾		
	▾		

Picklist

Irrecoverable debts
Purchases
Purchases ledger control
Sales
Sales ledger control
VAT control
Zoe Daniels

A new business has been started and a new set of accounts is to be opened. A partially completed journal to record the opening entries is shown below.

(b) **Complete the journal by showing whether each amount will be a debit or credit entry.**

Journal

Account name	Amount £	Debit ✓	Credit ✓
Cash at bank	1,090		
Capital	5,000		
Computer equipment	6,910		
Loan from bank	3,000		

Task 4 (10 marks)

This is a summary of transactions to be recorded in the VAT control account in June.

(a) **Show whether each transaction will be a debit or a credit entry in the VAT control account.**

Transactions	Amount £	Debit	Credit
VAT owing from HM Revenue and Customs at 1 June	2,055	☐	☐
VAT total in the sales daybook	5,820	☐	☐
VAT total in the sales returns daybook	493	☐	☐
VAT total in the purchases daybook	4,215	☐	☐
VAT total in the discounts allowed daybook	152	☐	☐
VAT total in the discounts received daybook	208	☐	☐
VAT total in the cash book for cash sales	804	☐	☐
VAT refund received from HM Revenue and Customs	2,055	☐	☐

At the end of July the VAT control account has debit entries amounting of £7,055 and credit entries amounting to £11,388.

The following transactions have not yet been recorded in the VAT control account.

- VAT total of £380 in the purchases returns daybook
- VAT of £195 on an irrecoverable debt written off.

(b) **What will be the balance brought down on the VAT control account after the transactions above have been recorded?**

Amount £	Debit	Credit
	☐	☐

Task 5 (14 marks)

These are the accounts in the sales ledger at 1 July.

Redlan plc

Details	Amount £	Details	Amount £
Balance b/f	8,927		

Patsy Perry

Details	Amount £	Details	Amount £
		Balance b/f	362

Annal Ltd

Details	Amount £	Details	Amount £
Balance b/f	14,066		

Samson and Dyer

Details	Amount £	Details	Amount £
Balance b/f	21,932		

(a) **What is the total of the balances in the sales ledger on 1 July?**

£ _____

The balance at the sales ledger control account on 1 July is £43,108.

(b) **What is the difference between the balance of the sales ledger control account and the total of the balances in the sales ledger you calculated in (a)?**

£ _____

(c) **Which TWO of the reasons below could explain the difference you calculated in (b)?**

Reasons	
Goods returned were entered twice in a customer's account in the sales ledger.	☐
Discounts allowed were not entered in the sales ledger control account.	☐
Goods sold were entered twice in a customers' account in the sales ledger.	☐
Goods returned were not entered in the sales ledger control account.	☐
Irrecoverable debts written off were entered twice in the sales ledger control account.	☐
A cheque received was entered twice in a customer's account in the sales ledger.	☐

This is a summary of transactions with credit suppliers during July.

Transactions	Amount £
Balance of payables at 1 July 20XX	38,677
Payments made by cheque	29,512
Goods purchased	32,619
Goods returned	4,037

(d) **Record these transaction in the purchases ledger control account and show the balance carried down.**

Purchases ledger control

Details	Amount £	Details	Amount £
▼		▼	
▼		▼	
▼		▼	
▼		▼	
▼		▼	
▼		▼	

Picklist

Balance b/d
Balance c/d
Bank
Discounts allowed
Discounts received
Purchases
Purchases returns
Sales
Sales returns

Task 6 (10 marks)

The bank statement and cash book for May are shown below.

Check the bank statement against the cash book and enter:

- **Any transactions into the cash book as needed**
- **The cash book balance carried down at 31 May and brought down at 1 June**

Bank statement

Date 20XX	Details	Paid out £	Paid in £	Balance £
01 May	Balance b/f			1,466 C
02 May	Bank interest		29	1,495 C
05 May	Cheque 011382	707		788 C
06 May	Cheque 011365	698		90 C
15 May	Counter credit		5,415	5,505 C
17 May	Khan and Wade – BACS		854	6,359 C
19 May	Cheque 011385	2,240		4,119 C
21 May	Cheque 011384	1,627		2,492 C
25 May	PQ Partners – SO	3,500		1,008 D
26 May	Counter credit		1,316	308 C
29 May	Cheque 011387	289		19 C

Cash book

Date 20XX	Details	Bank £	Date 20XX	Cheque number	Details	Bank £
1 May	Balance b/f	768	1 May	011382	Cully and Ball	707
15 May	Ballo plc	5,415	4 May	011383	Gaye Green	622
26 May	Heidi Chin	1,316	6 May	011384	KBC Ltd	1,627
	▼		10 May	011385	Farr traders	2,240
	▼		12 May	011386	Robson Ltd	525
	▼		16 May	011387	Lindy Lee	289
					▼	
	▼				▼	

Picklist

Balance b/d
Balance c/d
Ballo plc
Bank interest
Cheque 011365
Counter credit
Cully and Ball
Farr Traders
Gaye Green
Heidi Chin
KBC Ltd
Khan and Wade
Lindy Lee
PQ Partners
Robson Ltd

Task 7 (14 marks)

Below is the bank statement for July.

Bank statement

Date 20XX	Details	Paid out £	Paid in £	Balance £
01 Jul	Balance b/f			1,008 C
07 Jul	Cheque 014417	805		203 C
07 Jul	Counter credit		2,092	2,295 C
09 Jul	Cheque 014409	619		1,676 C
15 Jul	Cheque 014419	1,246		430 C
17 Jul	Counter credit		3,955	4,385 C
20 Jul	Cheque 014421	288		4,097 C
23 Jul	Counter credit		1,480	5,577 C
25 Jul	Cheque 014423	1,565		4,012 C
26 Jul	Cheque 014420	723		3,289 C

D = Debit C = Credit

The cash book and bank reconciliation statement for July have not yet been finalised.

(a) Identify the FOUR transactions that are included in the cash book but missing from the bank statement and complete the bank reconciliation statement as at 31 July.

Do not enter figures with minus signs or brackets in this task.

Bank reconciliation statement	£
Balance as per bank statement	
Add:	
▼	
▼	
Total to add	
Less:	
▼	
▼	
Total to subtract	
Balance as per cash book	

Picklist

Ali and May
Bron plc
Cheque 014409
Counter credit
GM Gray
Jasmine Jay
Kann plc
KJM Ltd
Larch Ltd
Ollie Wong
Peel Ltd
Slade plc
Tay Traders
Wilson Ltd

Cashbook

Date 20XX	Details	Bank £	Date 20XX	Cheque number	Details	Bank £
1 Jul	Balance b/f	389	3 Jul	014417	Ali and May	805
7 Jul	Slade plc	2,092	5 Jul	014418	Larch Ltd	771
9 Jul	Wilson Ltd	624	10 Jul	014419	Ollie Wong	1,246
17 Jul	Tay Traders	3,955	14 Jul	014420	KJM Ltd	723
23 Jul	Kann plc	1,480	16 Jul	014421	Bron plc	288
28 Jul	Jasmine Jay	495	18 Jul	014422	Peel Ltd	909
			21 Jul	014423	GM Gray	1,565

(b) Refer to the cash book in (a) and check that the bank statement has been correctly reconciled by calculating:

- The balance carried down
- The total of the bank columns after the balance carried down has been recorded.

Balance carried down £	Bank column totals £

Task 8 (14 marks)

A suspense account has been opened with a balance of £180.

The error has been identified as an entry made in the general ledger from the incorrectly totalled net column in the sales daybook shown below.

Sales daybook

Date 20XX	Details		Invoice number	Total £	VAT £	Net £
30 Jul	SM Barber		1170	528	88	440
30 Jul	Pastel Prints		1171	1,230	205	1,025
30 Jul	Hyffe Ltd		1172	936	156	780
	Totals			2,694	449	2,425

(a) Record the journal entries needed to:

- Remove the incorrect entry
- Record the correct entry
- Remove the suspense account balance

Do not enter a zero in unused debit or credit column cells.

Journal to remove the incorrect entry

Account name		Debit £	Credit £
	▼		

Picklist

Sales
Sales ledger control
Sales returns
Suspense
VAT control

Journal to record the correct entry

Account name		Debit £	Credit £
	▼		

Picklist

Sales
Sales ledger control
Sales returns
Suspense
VAT control

Journal to remove the suspense account balance

Account name	Debit £	Credit £
▼		

Picklist

Sales
Sales ledger control
Sales returns
Suspense
VAT control

Another error has been found in the general ledger. Entries to record cash drawings of £425 has been reversed.

(b) Record the journal entries needed to:

- Remove the incorrect entries
- Record the correct entries

Do not enter a zero in unused debit or credit column cells.

Journal to remove the incorrect entries

Account name	Debit £	Credit £
▼		
▼		

Picklist

Bank
Capital
Cash
Drawings

Journal to record the correct entries

Account name	Debit £	Credit £
▼		
▼		

Picklist

Bank
Capital
Cash
Drawings

Task 9 (10 marks)

The journal entries below have been prepared to correct an error.

Journal

Account name	Debit £	Credit £
Office furniture	1,476	
Suspense		1,476
Suspense	1,764	
Office furniture		1,764

Record the journal entries in the general ledger accounts below and show the balance carried down in the office furniture account.

Office furniture

Details	Amount £	Details	Amount £
Balance b/f	8,363	▼	
Bank	611	▼	
▼		▼	
▼		▼	
▼		▼	

Picklist

Balance b/d
Balance c/d
Bank
Office furniture
Suspense

Suspense

Details		Amount £	Details		Amount £
	▼		Balance b/d		288
	▼			▼	
	▼			▼	
		1,764			1,764

Picklist

Balance b/d
Balance c/d
Bank
Office furniture
Suspense

Task 10 (14 marks)

On 30 September a trial balance was extracted and did not balance. The debit column totalled £199,601 and the credit column totalled £200,827.

(a) **What entry is needed in the suspense account to balance the trial balance?**

Do not enter a zero in the unused column cell.

Account names	Debit £	Credit £
Suspense		

The journal entries to correct all the bookkeeping errors, and a list of balances as they appear in the trial balance, are shown below.

Journal

Account name	Debit ✓	Credit ✓
Office expenses	241	
Bank		241
Office expenses	241	
Bank		241

Account name	Debit ✓	Credit ✓
Fixtures and fittings	1,569	
Suspense		1,569
Suspense	343	
Rent received		343

(b) **Complete the table below to show:**

- **The balance of each account after the journal entries have been recorded**
- **Whether each balance will be a debit or credit entry in the trial balance, by ticking the appropriate column**

List of balances

Account name	Original balance £	New balance £	Debit ✓	Credit ✓
Office expense	1,967			
Bank (overdraft)	1,076			
Fixtures and fittings	12,334			
Rent received	602			

On 31 October a partially prepared trial balance had debit balances totalling £210,678 and credit balances totalling £208,911. The accounts below have not yet been entered into the trial balance.

(c) **Complete the table below to show whether each balance will be a debit or credit entry in the trial balance.**

Account names	Balance £	Debit ✓	Credit ✓
VAT control (owing to HM Revenue and Customs)	12,053		
Sales returns	4,671		
Drawing	5,615		

(d) **What will be the totals of each column of the trial balance after the balances in (c) have been entered?**

Account name	Debit £	Credit £
Totals		

AAT AQ2016 SAMPLE ASSESSMENT
BOOKKEEPING CONTROLS

ANSWERS

Bookkeeping Controls
AAT sample assessment

Task 1 (12 marks)

(a)

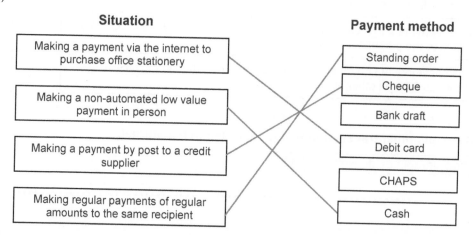

Situation

| | **Payment method** |

Making a payment via the internet to purchase office stationery

Making a non-automated low value payment in person

Making a payment by post to a credit supplier

Making regular payments of regular amounts to the same recipient

Standing order

Cheque

Bank draft

Debit card

CHAPS

Cash

(b)

Payment method
Credit card ▼
Cheque ▼

(c)

Error	Effect on trial balance
A cash sale has been recorded in the sales and VAT control accounts only.	Will cause an imbalance ▼
The purchase of a new computer has been recorded in the office expenses account. All other entries were correct.	Will not cause an imbalance ▼
A BACS payment to a credit supplier was debited to the bank account and credited to the purchases ledger control account.	Will not cause an imbalance ▼
A cash payment of £56 for stationery has been recorded in the cash account as £65. All other entries were correct.	Will cause an imbalance ▼

(d)

Error	
A cash sale has been recorded in the sales and VAT control accounts only.	☐
The purchase of a new computer has been recorded in the office expenses account. All other entries were correct.	☑
A BACS payment to a credit supplier was debited to the bank account and credited to the purchases ledger control account.	☐
A cash payment of £56 for stationery has been recorded in the cash account as £65. All other entries were correct.	☐

The correction of errors in a bookkeeping system is recorded in the journal.

(e) **Select one other transaction that is recorded in the journal.**

Irrecoverable debts written off ▼

Task 2 (12 marks)

Journal to record the net wages paid to employees

Account name		Debit £	Credit £
Wages control	▼	52,926	
Bank	▼		52,926

Journal to record the HM Revenue and Customs liability

Account name		Debit £	Credit £
Wages control	▼	17,004	
HM Revenue and Customs	▼		17,004

Journal to record the trade union liability

Account name		Debit £	Credit £
Wages control	▼	630	
Trade union	▼		630

Task 3 (10 marks)

(a) Journal

Account name		Debit £	Credit £
Irrecoverable debts	▼	1,460	
VAT control	▼	292	
Sales ledger control	▼		1,752

(b) Journal

Account name	Amount £	Debit £	Credit £
Cash at bank	1,090	✓	
Capital	5,000		✓
Computer equipment	6,910	✓	
Loan from bank	3,000		✓

Task 4 (10 marks)

(a)

Account name	Amount £	Debit	Credit
VAT owing from HM Revenue and Customs at 1 June	2,055	✓	☐
VAT total in the sales daybook	5,820	☐	✓
VAT total in the sales returns daybook	493	✓	☐
VAT total in the purchases daybook	4,215	✓	☐
VAT total in the discounts allowed daybook	152	✓	☐
VAT total in the discounts received daybook	208	☐	✓
VAT total in the cash book for cash sales	804	☐	✓
VAT refund received from HM Revenue and Customs	2,055	☐	✓

(b)

Amount £	Debit	Credit
4,518	☐	✓

....

Task 5 (14 marks)

(a) £ 44,563

(b) £ 1,455

(c)

Reasons	
Goods returned were entered twice in a customer's account in the sales ledger.	☐
Discounts allowed were not entered in the sales ledger control account.	☐
Goods sold were entered twice in a customers' account in the sales ledger.	✓
Goods returned were not entered in the sales ledger control account.	☐
Irrecoverable debts written off were entered twice in the sales ledger control account.	✓
A cheque received was entered twice in a customer's account in the sales ledger.	☐

(d) **Purchases ledger control**

Details		Amount £	Details		Amount £
Bank	▼	29,512	Balance b/d	▼	38,677
Purchases returns	▼	4,037	Purchases	▼	32,619
Balance c/d	▼	37,747		▼	
	▼			▼	
	▼			▼	
	▼			▼	
		71,296			71,296

....

Task 6 (10 marks)

Cash book

Date 20XX	Details	Bank £	Date 20XX	Cheque number	Details	Bank £
1 May	Balance b/f	768	1 May	011382	Cully and Ball	707
15 May	Ballo plc	5,415	4 May	011383	Gaye Green	622
26 May	Heidi Chin	1,316	6 May	011384	KBC Ltd	1,627
2 May	Bank interest ▼	29	10 May	011385	Farr traders	2,240
17 May	Khan and Wade ▼	854	12 May	011386	Robson Ltd	525
31 May	Balance c/d ▼	1,128	16 May	011387	Lindy Lee	289
			25 May		PQ Partners ▼	3,500
		9,510				9,510
	▼		1 Jun		Balance b/d ▼	1,128

··

Task 7 (14 marks)

(a)

Bank reconciliation statement		£
Balance as per bank statement		3,289
Add:		
Wilson Ltd	▼	624
Jasmine Jay	▼	495
Total to add		1,119
Less:		
Larch Ltd	▼	771
Peel Ltd	▼	909
Total to subtract		1,680
Balance as per cash book		2,728

(b)

Balance carried down £	Bank column totals £
2,728	9,035

Task 8 (14 marks)

(a)

Account name		Debit £	Credit £
Sales	▼	2,425	

Journal to record the correct entry

Account name		Debit £	Credit £
Sales	▼		2,245

Journal to remove the suspense account balance

Account name		Debit £	Credit £
Suspense	▼		180

(b)   Journal to remove the incorrect entries

Account name		Debit £	Credit £
Drawings	▼	425	
Cash	▼		425

Journal to record the correct entries

Account name		Debit £	Credit £
Drawings	▼	425	
Cash	▼		425

Task 9 (10 marks)

Office furniture

Details		Amount £	Details		Amount £
Balance b/f		8,363	Suspense	▼	1,764
Bank		611	Balance c/d	▼	8,686
Suspense	▼	1,476		▼	
		10,450			10,450

Suspense

Details		Amount £	Details		Amount £
Office furniture	▼	1,764	Balance b/d		288
	▼		Office furniture	▼	1,476
		1,764			1,764

Task 10 (14 marks)

(a)

Account names	Debit £	Credit £
Suspense	1,226	

(b)

Account names	Original balance £	New balance £	Debit in trial balance	Credit in trial balance
Office expense	1,967	2,449	✓	☐
Bank (overdraft)	1,076	1,558	☐	✓
Fixtures and fittings	12,334	13,903	✓	☐
Rent received	602	945	☐	✓

(c)

Account names	Balance £	Debit in trial balance	Credit in trial balance
VAT control (owing to HM Revenue and Customs)	12,053	☐	✓
Sales returns	4,671	✓	☐
Drawing	5,615	✓	☐

(d)

Account name	Debit £	Credit £
Totals	220,964	220,964

BPP PRACTICE ASSESSMENT 1
BOOKKEEPING CONTROLS

Time allowed: 2 hours

Bookkeeping Controls
BPP practice assessment 1

Each task is independent. You will not need to refer to your answers to previous tasks.

Read every task carefully to make sure you understand what is required.

Where the date is relevant, it is given in the task data.

Both minus signs and brackets can be used to indicate negative numbers **unless** task instructions say otherwise.

You must use a full stop to indicate a decimal point. For example, write 100.57 **not** 100,57 **or** 100 57.

You may use a comma to indicate a number in the thousands, but you don't have to. For example, 10000 and 10,000 are both OK.

Other indicators are not compatible with the computer-marked system.

Complete all 10 tasks.

You are employed by the business, Russell Hardware, as a bookkeeper.

- Russell Hardware uses a manual accounting system.

- Double entry takes place in the general ledger. Individual accounts of trade receivables and trade payables are kept in the sales and purchases ledgers as subsidiary accounts.

- The cash book and petty cash book should be treated as part of the double entry system unless the task instructions state otherwise.

- The VAT rate is 20%.

Task 1

(a) **Match each situation with the most appropriate payment method by selecting from the picklist.**

Situation	Payment method
Making a payment via the internet to purchase office supplies	▼
Making a non-automated low value payment in person	▼
Making a payment to a supplier by post	▼
Making regular payments of set amounts to the same recipient	▼

Picklist

Bank draft
Cash
CHAPS
Cheque
Debit card
Standing order

(b) **Show which TWO of the payment methods below will reduce funds in the payer's bank balance on the date of payment, by ticking the appropriate boxes.**

Payment method	Reduce funds on the date of payment ✓
Credit card	
Direct debit	
Cash	
CHAPS	
Cheque	

(c) **Show which TWO of the errors below will cause an imbalance in the trial balance by ticking the appropriate boxes**

Error	Imbalance in the trial balance ✓
The purchase of new desks for the office has been recorded in the office expenses account. All other entries were correct	
A cash payment of £64 for stationery has been recorded in the cash account as £46. All other entries were correct	
Recording a credit note from a supplier on the debit side of the purchases ledger control account and the debit side of the purchase returns account	
Recording a purchase from a credit supplier for £5,000 as £500 in both the purchases and the purchase ledger account (no VAT)	

(d) **Show which ONE error is an error of principle, by selecting the appropriate box in the table below.**

Error	Error of principal ✓
The purchase of a new computer has been recorded in the office expenses account. All other entries were correct	
A cash sale has been recorded in the sales and VAT control accounts only	
A cash payment of £64 for stationery has been recorded in the cash account as £46. All other entries were correct	
A BACS payment to a credit supplier was debited to the bank account and credited to the purchases ledger control account	

The correction of errors in a bookkeeping system is recorded in the journal.

(e) **Select one other transaction that is recorded in the journal.**

Statements	✓
Prompt payment discounts received	
Interest received from the bank	
Irrecoverable debts written off	
Re-imbursement of petty cash	

Task 2

Russell Hardware pays its employees by BACS direct credit transfer every month and maintains a wages control account.

A summary of last month's payroll transactions is shown below:

Item	£
Gross wages	7,450
Employees' NI	682
Income tax	1,204
Trade union subscriptions	90
Employer's NI	809

Record the journal entries needed in the general ledger to:

(a)   Record the net wages paid to the employees

Account name		Debit £	Credit £
	▼		
	▼		

(b)   Record the HM Revenue and Customs liability

Account name		Debit £	Credit £
	▼		
	▼		

(c)   Record the trade union liability

Account name		Debit £	Credit £
	▼		
	▼		

Picklist

Bank
Employees' NI
Employer's NI
HM Revenue and Customs
Income tax
Trade union subscription
Wages control
Wages expense

Task 3

This is a customer's account in the sales ledger.

Bryson Construction

Date 20XX	Details	Amount £	Date 20XX	Details	Amount £
01 Jan	Balance b/f	450	4 Jan	Credit note 45	35
15 Jan	Invoice 951	785	17 Jan	Credit note 46	210

The customer has now ceased trading owing the amount outstanding which includes VAT.

(a) Record the journal entries needed in the general ledger to write off the net amount and the VAT.

		Debit £	Credit £
	▼		
	▼		
	▼		

Picklist

Irrecoverable debt expense
Sales ledger control
VAT control

A new business has been started and a new set of accounts are to be opened. A partially completed journal to record the opening entries is shown below.

(b) Complete the journal by ticking either the debit or credit column.

Account name	Amount £	Debit ✓	Credit ✓
Cash at bank	2,400		
Capital	6,000		
Loan from bank	1,200		
Computer equipment	4,800		

Task 4

This is a summary of transactions to be recorded in the VAT control account in April.

(a) **Show whether each transaction will be a debit or a credit entry in the VAT control account by ticking the relevant box in the debit or credit column**

Details	Amount £	Debit ✓	Credit ✓
VAT owing from HM Revenue and Customs at 1 April	1,604		
VAT total in the sales daybook	4,750		
VAT total in the sales returns daybook	320		
VAT total in the purchases daybook	3,710		
VAT total in the discounts allowed daybook	780		
VAT total in the discounts received daybook	150		
VAT total in the cash book for cash purchases	840		
VAT refund received from HM Revenue and Customs	1,604		

At the end of July the VAT control account has debit entries amount to £6,410 and credit entries amount to £10,900.

The following transactions have not yet been recorded in the VAT control account:

- VAT total of £395 in the purchases returns daybook
- VAT of £225 on an irrecoverable debt written off

(b) **What will be the balance brought down on the VAT control account after the transactions above have been recorded?**

Amount £	Debit ✓	Credit ✓

BPP
LEARNING MEDIA

Task 5

These are the accounts in the sales ledger at 1 October.

Charlotte Ltd

Details	Amount £	Details	Amount £
Balance b/f	8,700		

Anne plc

Details	Amount £	Details	Amount £
Balance b/f	21,500		

Emily & Co

Details	Amount £	Details	Amount £
		Balance b/f	450

Haworths

Details	Amount £	Details	Amount £
Balance b/f	11,200		

(a) What is the total of the balances in the sales ledger on 1 October?

£ [   ]

The balance of the sales ledger control account on 1 October is £41,590.

(b) What is the difference between the balance of the sales ledger control account and the total of the balances in the sales ledger you calculated in (a)?

£ [   ]

(c) Which TWO of the reasons below could explain the difference you calculated in (b). Tick the relevant options in the table below?

Reasons	✓
Goods returned may have been entered in the customer's account in the sales ledger twice	
Discounts allowed were entered in the sales ledger control account only	
Goods returned were omitted from the sales ledger control account	
Goods sold were entered twice in a customer's account in the sales ledger	
A cheque received was entered in the sales ledger control account twice	

This is a summary of transactions with credit suppliers during May 20XX.

Transactions	Amount £
Balance of payables at 1 May 20XX	27,500
Payments made by cheque	23,200
Goods purchased	13,800
Goods returned	6,800

(d) **Record these transactions in the purchases ledger control account and show the balance carried down.**

Purchases ledger control

	Amount £		Amount £
▼		▼	
▼		▼	
▼			

Picklist

Balance b/f
Balance c/d
Bank
Discount received
Purchases
Purchases returns

Task 6

The bank statement and cash book for December are shown below

Required

Check the bank statement against the cash book and enter:

- **Any transactions into the cash book as needed**

- **The cash book balance carried down at 23 December and brought down at 24 December**

Enter dates in the format "XX Dec".

Bank statement

Date 20XX	Details	Paid out £	Paid in £	Balance £
01 Dec	Balance b/f			5,230 C
05 Dec	Counter credit Percival Ltd		8,560	13,790 C
10 Dec	Cheque 04256	400		13,390 C
13 Dec	Cheque 04257	690		12,700 C
14 Dec	Direct Debit Greenville DC	750		11,950 C
16 Dec	Cheque 04258	2,754		9,196 C
20 Dec	Counter credit: Bardier Bricks		5,500	14,696 C
21 Dec	Direct Debit Triggers Ltd	325		14,371 C
22 Dec	Cheque No 04260	850		13,521 C
23 Dec	Bank charges	25		13,496 C
23 Dec	Bank interest		15	13,511 C

D=Debit C=Credit

Cash book

Date 20XX	Details	Bank £	Date 20XX	Cheque number	Details	Bank £
01 Dec	Balance b/f	5,230	01 Dec	04256	Jacksons Ltd	400
20 Dec	Bardier Bricks Ltd	5,500	01 Dec	04257	Ristov & co	690
21 Dec	Darlingfords	4,650	07 Dec	04258	ARP Ltd	2,754
22 Dec	Scotts	3,755	08 Dec	04259	Tolkens	1,450
	▼		15 Dec	04260	Loose Chips Co	850
	▼		22 Dec	04261	SM Griggs	312
					▼	
					▼	
					▼	
					▼	
	▼				▼	

Picklist

ARP Ltd
Balance b/d
Balance c/d
Bank charges
Bank interest
Bardier Bricks
Darlingfords
Greenville DC
Jacksons Ltd
Loose chips Ltd
Percival Ltd
Ristov & Co
Scotts
SM Griggs
Tolkens
Triggers Ltd

Task 7

Below is the bank statement for March.

Date 20XX		Paid out £	Paid in £	Balance £
01 Mar	Balance b/f			3,460 C
05 Mar	Cheque 1165	465		2,995 C
12 Mar	Cheque 1167	7,200		4,205 D
15 Mar	GreenBee		9,460	5,255 C
16 Mar	Cheque 1166	533		4,722 C
23 Mar	Port Cookers		7,000	11,722 C
24 Mar	Cheque No 1169	2,400		9,322 C
26 Mar	Bank charges	25		9,297 C
28 Mar	Bank interest		27	9,324 C

D = Debit C = Credit

Bank reconciliation statement

(a) Cash book

Date 20XX		Bank £	Date 20XX	Cheque number	Details	Bank £
01 Mar	Balance b/f	3,460	02 Mar	1165	Bobbin & Co	465
10 Mar	GreenBee	9,460	03 Mar	1166	Freddies Ltd	533
14 Mar	Port Cookers	7,000	07 Mar	1167	Irons	7,200
21 Mar	Kitchen Co	3,452	05 Mar	1168	Jerry & Co	2,500
23 Mar	Nigella's	2,468	15 Mar	1169	P Smith	2,400
26 Mar	Bank interest	27	23 Mar	1170	J Frost	362
	▼		28 Mar		Bank charges	25
					▼	
	▼				▼	

Picklist

Balance b/d
Balance c/d

The cash book and bank reconciliation statement for March have not been finalised.

Identify the four transactions that are included in the cash book but are missing from the bank statement and complete the bank reconciliation statement as at 31 March.

Note. Do not make any entries in the shaded boxes.

Bank reconciliation statement		£
Balance per bank statement		
Add:		
	▼	
	▼	
Total to add		
Less:		
	▼	
	▼	
Total to subtract		
Balance as per cash book		

Picklist

Balance b/d
Balance c/d
Bank charges
Bank interest
Bobbin & Co
Freddies Ltd
GreenBee
Irons
J Frost
Jerry & Co
Kitchen Co
Nigella's
P Smith
Port Cookers

(b) Refer to the cash book in (a) and check that the bank statement has been correctly reconciled by calculating:

- The balance carried down

- The total of each of the bank columns after the balance carried down has been recorded

Balance carried down £	Bank column totals £

Task 8

A suspense account has been opened with a balance of £118.

The error has been identified as an entry made in the general ledger from the incorrectly totalled net column in the sales day book, as shown below.

Sales day book

Date 20XX	Details	Invoice number	Total £	VAT £	Net £
31 Oct	Drury Ltd	144	288	48	240
31 Oct	Davenport	145	1,740	290	1,450
31 Oct	Williams & Co	146	3,174	529	2,645
	Totals		5,202	867	4,453

(a) Record the journal entries needed to:

- Remove the incorrect entry
- Record the correct entry
- Remove the suspense account balance

Journal to remove the incorrect entry

Account name	Amount £	Debit ✓	Credit ✓
▼			

Journal to record the correct entry

Account name	Amount £	Debit ✓	Credit ✓
▼			

Journal to remove the suspense account balance

Account name		Amount £	Debit ✓	Credit ✓
	▼			

Picklist

Davenport
Drury Ltd
Sales
Sales ledger control
Suspense
VAT
Williams & Co

Another error has been found in the general ledger. An entry to record a purchase of £550 relating to marketing expenses has been recorded as £505 on the marketing expense account.

(b)   Record the journal entries needed to:

- **Remove the incorrect entry**
- **Record the correct entries**

Do not enter a zero in unused debit or credit column cells.

Journal to remove the incorrect entries

		Amount £	Debit ✓	Credit ✓
	▼			
	▼			

Journal to record the correct entry

		Amount £	Debit ✓	Credit ✓
	▼			
	▼			

Picklist

Marketing expense account
Suspense

Task 9

The journal entries below have been prepared to correct an error.

Journal

Account name	Debit £	Credit £
Heat & Light	1,650	
Suspense		1,650
Suspense	1,560	
Heat & Light		1,560

Post the journal entries in the general ledger accounts below and show the balance carried down in the heat and light account.

Heat & Light

Details	Amount £	Details	Amount £
Balance b/f	4,760	▼	
▼		▼	

Suspense

Details	Amount £	Details	Amount £
Balance b/f	90	▼	
▼		▼	

Picklist

Balance b/f
Balance c/d
Heat & Light
Suspense

Task 10

On 28 February a trial balance was extracted and did not balance. The debit column totaled £448,100 and the credit column totaled £450,100.

(a) **What entry would be made in the suspense account to balance the trial balance? Select whether this would be a debit or a credit.**

	Amount £	Debit ✓	Credit ✓
Suspense			

The journal entries to correct all the bookkeeping errors, and a list of balances as they appear in the trial balance, are shown below

Account name	Debit ✓	Credit ✓
Suspense	200	
Bank		200
Heat & Light	200	
Bank		200

Account name	Debit ✓	Credit ✓
Rent paid	2,500	
Suspense		2,500
Suspense	300	
Advertising		300

(b) **Complete the table below to show:**

- **The balance of each account after the journal entries have been recorded**
- **Whether each balance will be a debit or credit entry in the trial balance**

List of balances

Account name	Original balance £	New balance £	Debit ✓	Credit ✓
Heat & Light	800			
Bank (debit)	4,500			
Advertising	960			
Rent paid	6,500			

On 30 April a partially prepared trial balance had debit balances totalling £171,600 and credit balances totalling £168,200. The accounts below have not yet been entered into the trial balance.

(c) Complete the table below to show whether each balance will be a debit or credit entry in the trial balance.

Account name	Balance £	Debit ✓	Credit ✓
VAT control (owing to HM Revenue and Customs)	2,800		
Loan	9,000		
Computer equipment	8,400		

(d) What will be the totals of each column of the trial balance after the balances in (c) have been entered?

Account name	Debit £	Credit £
Totals		

BPP PRACTICE ASSESSMENT 1
BOOKKEEPING CONTROLS

ANSWERS

Bookkeeping Controls
BPP practice assessment 1

Task 1

(a)

Situation	Payment method
Making a payment via the internet to purchase office supplies	Debit card
Making a non-automated low value payment in person	Cash
Making a payment to a supplier by post	Cheque
Making regular payments of set amounts to the same recipient	Standing order

(b)

Payment method	Reduce funds on the date of payment ✓
Credit card	
Direct debit	✓
Cash	
CHAPS	✓
Cheque	

(c)

Error	Imbalance in the trial balance ✓
The purchase of new desks for the office has been recorded in the office expenses account. All other entries were correct	
A cash payment of £64 for stationery has been recorded in the cash account as £46. All other entries were correct	✓
Recording a credit note from a supplier on the debit side of the purchases ledger control account and the debit side of the purchase returns account.	✓
Recording a purchase from a credit supplier for £5,000 as £500 in both the purchases and the purchase ledger account (no VAT)	

Errors one and four will not show an imbalance in the trial balance as equal debits and credits have been posted, but not to the correct accounts. These will not be detected in the trial balance

Error two has shown an imbalance as the debits and credits do not match, so the trial balance will show the error.

Error three has two debit entries, therefore, there will be an imbalance in the trial balance.

(d)

Error	Error of principal ✓
The purchase of a new computer has been recorded in the office expenses account. All other entries were correct	✓
A cash sale has been recorded in the sales and VAT control accounts only	
A cash payment of £64 for stationery has been recorded in the cash account as £46. All other entries were correct	
A BACS payment to a credit supplier was debited to the bank account and credited to the purchases ledger control account	

An error of principle occurs where the bookkeeper enters a transaction in the wrong type of account. Only error one is posted to the incorrect account, the others are incorrect postings to the correct accounts (such as the payment to the supplier being posted as a credit, whereas it should have been a debit posting)

(e)

Statements	
Prompt payment discounts received	
Interest received from the bank	
Irrecoverable debts written off	✓
Re-imbursement of petty cash	

Task 2

(a) **Journal to record the net wages paid to the employees**

Account name	Debit £	Credit £
Wages control	5,474	
Bank		5,474

(b) **Journal to record the HM Revenue and Customs liability**

Account name	Debit £	Credit £
Wages control	2,695	
HMRC		2,695

(c) **Journal to record the trade union liability**

Account name	Debit £	Credit £
Wages control	90	
Trade union subscription		90

Task 3

(a)

	Debit £	Credit £
Irrecoverable debt expense	825	
Sales ledger control		990
VAT control	165	

(b)

	Amount £	Debit ✓	Credit ✓
Cash at bank	2,400	✓	
Capital	6,000		✓
Loan from bank	1,200		✓
Computer equipment	4,800	✓	

Task 4

(a)

Details	Amount £	Debit ✓	Credit ✓
VAT owing from HM Revenue and Customs at 1 April	1,604	✓	
VAT total in the sales daybook	4,750		✓
VAT total in the sales returns daybook	320	✓	
VAT total in the purchases daybook	3,710	✓	
VAT total in the discounts allowed daybook	780	✓	
VAT total in the discounts received daybook	150		✓
VAT total in the cash book for cash purchases	840	✓	
VAT refund received from HM Revenue and Customs	1,604		✓

(b)

Amount £	Debit ✓	Credit ✓
4,660		✓

The requirement asks for the balance b/d. This is on the opposite side to the balance c/d and completes the double entry.

....

Task 5

(a)

£	40,950

(b)

£	640

(c)

Reasons	✓
Goods returned may have been entered in the customer's account in the sales ledger twice	✓
Discounts allowed were entered in the sales ledger control account only	
Goods returned were omitted from the sales ledger control account.	✓
Goods sold were entered twice in a customer's account in the sales ledger.	
A cheque received was entered in the sales ledger control account twice	

(d)

Purchases ledger control

Details	Amount £	Details	Amount £
Bank	23,200	Balance b/f	27,500
Purchases returns	6,800	Purchases	13,800
Balance c/d	11,300		
	41,300		41,300

Task 6

Cash book

Date 20XX	Details	Bank £	Date 20XX	Cheque number	Details	Bank £
01 Dec	Balance b/f	5,230	01 Dec	04256	Jacksons Ltd	400
20 Dec	Bardier Bricks Ltd	5,500	01 Dec	04257	Ristov & co	690
21 Dec	Darlingfords	4,650	07 Dec	04258	ARP Ltd	2,754
22 Dec	Scotts	3,755	08 Dec	04259	Tolkens	1,450
05 Dec	**Percival Ltd**	**8,560**	15 Dec	04260	Loose Chips Co	850
23 Dec	**Bank interest**	**15**	22 Dec	04261	SM Griggs	312
			23 Dec		**Bank charges**	**25**
			14 Dec	**DD**	**Greenville DC**	**750**
			21 Dec	**DD**	**Triggers Ltd**	**325**
					Balance c/d	**20,154**
		27,710				27,710
	Balance b/d	**20,154**				

In order to reconcile the adjusted cash book with the bank statement via the bank reconciliation statement, the first step is to review both documents and identify the items which are already entered in the cash book and have cleared the bank statement.

Cash book

The opening balances of the cash book and bank statement are the same, meaning there are no entries relating to a prior period reconciliation.

After the crossing-off exercise, note that the bank statement had three payments that need to be recorded in the cash book (£25, £750 and £325) and two deposits (£8,560 and £15). Remember that withdrawals are a credit in the cash book and deposits are a debit.

To balance off the cash book both the debt and credit sides are totalled. The debit column is higher, so that total is put at the bottom of BOTH columns. The balancing figure on the credit side of £20,154 becomes the balance c/d. It is brought down on the opposite side of the account (the debit side), ready for the start of the new period.

Task 7

(a) Cash book

Date 20XX	Details	Bank £	Date 20XX	Cheque number	Details	Bank £
01 Mar	Balance b/f	3,460	02 Mar	1165	Bobbin & Co	465
10 Mar	GreenBee	9,460	03 Mar	1166	Freddies Ltd	533
14 Mar	Port Cookers	7,000	07 Mar	1167	Irons	7,200
21 Mar	Kitchen Co	3,452	05 Mar	1168	Jerry & Co	2,500
23 Mar	Nigella's	2,468	15 Mar	1169	P Smith	2,400
26 Mar	Bank interest	27	23 Mar	1170	J Frost	362
			28 Mar		Bank charges	25
			31 Mar		Balance c/d	12,382
		25,867				25,867
1 Apr	Balance b/d	12,382				

Bank reconciliation statement	£
Balance per bank statement	9,324
Add:	
Nigella's	2,468
Kitchen Co	3,452
Total to add	5,920
Less:	
Jerry & Co	2,500
J Frost	362
Total to subtract	2,862
Balance as per cash book	12,382

(b)

Balance carried down £	Bank column totals £
12,382	25,867

Task 8

(a)

Account name	Amount £	Debit ✓	Credit ✓
Sales	4,453	✓	

Account name	Amount £	Debit ✓	Credit ✓
Sales	4,335		✓

Account name	Amount £	Debit ✓	Credit ✓
Suspense	118		✓

(b)

Account name	Amount £	Debit ✓	Credit ✓
Marketing expense account	505		✓
Suspense	505	✓	

Account name	Amount £	Debit ✓	Credit ✓
Marketing expense account	550	✓	
Suspense	550		✓

Task 9

Heat & Light

Details	Amount £	Details	Amount £
Balance b/f	4,760	Suspense	1,560
Suspense	1,650	Balance c/d	4,850
	6,410		6,410

Suspense

Details	Amount £	Details	Amount £
Balance b/f	90	Heat & Light	1,650
Heat & Light	1,560	Balance c/d	–
	1,650		1,650

Task 10

(a)

Account name	Amount £	Debit ✓	Credit ✓
Suspense	2,000	✓	

(b)

	Original balance £	New balance £	Debit ✓	Credit ✓
Heat & Light	800	1,000	✓	
Bank (debit)	4,500	4,100	✓	
Advertising	960	660	✓	
Rent paid	6,500	9,000	✓	

(c)

Account name	Balance £	Debit ✓	Credit ✓
VAT control (owing to HM Revenue and Customs)	2,800		✓
Loan	9,000		✓
Computer equipment	8,400	✓	

(d)

Account name	Debit £	Credit £
Totals	180,000	180,000

BPP PRACTICE ASSESSMENT 2
BOOKKEEPING CONTROLS

Time allowed: 2 hours

Bookkeeping Controls
BPP practice assessment 2

Each task is independent. You will not need to refer to your answers to previous tasks.

Read every task carefully to make sure you understand what is required.

Where the date is relevant, it is given in the task data.

Both minus signs and brackets can be used to indicate negative numbers **unless** task instructions say otherwise.

You must use a full stop to indicate a decimal point. For example, write 100.57 **not** 100,57 **or** 100 57.

You may use a comma to indicate a number in the thousands, but you don't have to. For example, 10000 and 10,000 are both OK.

Other indicators are not compatible with the computer-marked system.

Complete all 10 tasks.

You are employed by the business, Jones & Co, as a bookkeeper.

- Jones & Co uses a manual accounting system.

- Double entry takes place in the general ledger. Individual accounts of trade receivables and trade payables are kept in the sales and purchases ledgers as subsidiary accounts.

- The cash book and petty cash book should be treated as part of the double entry system unless the task instructions state otherwise.

- The VAT rate is 20%.

Task 1

(a) Identify the effect the different payment methods have on the bank balance.

Payment Method	Reduce funds on the date of payment ✓	Reduce funds at a later date ✓
Credit card		
Cash withdrawal from the bank account		
BACS direct credit		
Cheque		
CHAPS		

(b) Select the most appropriate method of payment for the following transactions

Situation	Payment method
Payment of an invoice to a supplier where goods were purchased on credit. The payment is due today and is for £1,300	▼
Purchasing tea and coffee supplies for the office from the local supermarket	▼
Ordering new printer paper online	▼
Payment of local business rates on a monthly basis for the same value each month (£250)	▼
Payment of legal fees to the company's solicitor for general business advice (£550)	▼

Picklist

Cash
CHAPS
Cheque
Debit card
Direct Debit
Faster payment

(c) Show which of the errors below are, or are not, disclosed by the trial balance.

Error in the general ledger	Error disclosed by the trial balance ✓	Error NOT disclosed by the trial balance ✓
Making a transposition error in the debit entry from the journal in the general ledger but not in the credit entry		
Recording a sale to a customer for £75 cash (no VAT) as £57 in both the cash account and the sales account		
Recording a payment for a cash purchase (no VAT) in the trade payables column of the cash book		
Recording discount allowed to a customer on the debit side of the discount allowed account and the debit side of the sales ledger control account		
Recording a payment to a supplier on the credit side of the supplier's purchases ledger account		
Recording a sales return by debiting the sales ledger control account and crediting the sales returns account		

One of the errors in (c) above can be classified as an error of reversal of entries.

(d) Show which error is an error of reversal of entries.

Error in the general ledger	✓
Making a transposition error in the debit entry from the journal in the general ledger but not in the credit entry	
Recording a sale to a customer for £75 cash (no VAT) as £57 in both the cash account and the sales account	
Recording a payment for a cash purchase (no VAT) in the trade payables column of the cash book	
Recording discount allowed to a customer on the debit side of the discount allowed account and the debit side of the sales ledger control account	
Recording a payment to a supplier on the credit side of the supplier's purchases ledger account	
Recording a sales return by debiting the sales ledger control account and crediting the sales returns account	

Task 2

This is a summary of transactions to be recorded in the VAT control account in March.

(a) Show whether each transaction will be a debit or a credit entry in the VAT control account.

Details	Amount £	Debit ✓	Credit ✓
VAT owing to HM Revenue and Customs at 1 March	2,300		
VAT total in the sales daybook	5,320		
VAT total in the sales returns daybook	410		
VAT total in the purchases daybook	3,100		
VAT total in the discounts allowed daybook	250		
VAT total in the discounts received daybook	170		
VAT total in the cash book for cash sales	900		
VAT payment sent to HM Revenue and Customs	2,300		

(b) **What is the VAT balance at 31 March?**

Amount £	Debit ✓	Credit ✓

(c) **One of Jones & Co's customers, Jenson Ltd, has ceased trading owing the company £500 plus VAT. Record the journal entries needed in the general ledger to write off the net amount and the VAT.**

Account name		Amount £	Debit ✓	Credit ✓
	▼			
	▼			
	▼			

Picklist

Irrecoverable debts
Jenson Ltd
Jones & Co
Purchases
Purchases ledger control
Sales
Sales ledger control
VAT control

Task 3

The following is an extract from Jones & Co's books of prime entry.

Sales day book

Details	Gross £	VAT £	Net £
Q1	64,260	10,710	53,550

Purchases day book

	Gross £	VAT £	Net £
Q1	19,530	3,255	16,275

Sales returns day book

Details	Gross £	VAT £	Net £
Q1	3,360	560	2,800

Purchase returns day book

	Gross £	VAT £	Net £
Q1	1,302	217	1,085

There were also cash sales made of £1,008 (including VAT) during the quarter

(a) **What will be the entries in the VAT control account to record the VAT transactions in the quarter?**

VAT control

Details	Amount £	Details	Amount £
▼		▼	
▼		▼	
▼		▼	

Picklist

Cash book
Cash sales
Purchases
Purchases day book
Purchases returns
Purchases returns day book
Sales
Sales day book
Sales returns
Sales returns day book
VAT control

(b) The VAT return must now be completed. What is the balance owing to or from HM Revenue and Customs for the period?

Amount £	Amount due from HMRC ✓	Amount owed to HMRC ✓

(c) Which of the following TWO statements are true

	✓
The VAT control account is used to establish any balance due to or reclaimable from HMRC	
Payments to HMRC in respect of VAT owed are debited to the cash book and credited to the VAT control account	
The balance b/d on the VAT control account is the amount owed to (credit balance) or refundable by (debit balance) HMRC	
A return on sales (where VAT is charged) increases the VAT liability in the VAT control account	

Task 4

These are the accounts in the sales ledger at 1 January.

Sukhi Ltd

Details	Amount £	Details	Amount £
Balance b/f	1,560		

Ayesha plc

Details	Amount £	Details	Amount £
Balance b/f	4,790		

Sinead & Co

Details	Amount £	Details	Amount £
		Balance b/f	890

Iona's Pebbles Limited

Details	Amount £	Details	Amount £
Balance b/f	7,250		

(a) **What is the total of the balances in the sales ledger on 1 January?**

£ [ ]

The balance of the sales ledger control account on 1 January is £12,600.

(b) **What is the difference between the balance of the sales ledger control account and the total of the balances in the sales ledger you calculated in (a)?**

£ [ ]

(c) **Which ONE of the reasons below could explain the difference you calculated in (b) by ticking the appropriate answer in the table below?**

Reasons	✓
A payment from a customer was allocated against the wrong customer	
Discounts allowed were not entered in the sales ledger control account	
Goods sold were entered twice in the sales ledger control account	
Goods returned were omitted from the sales ledger.	

(d) Another error is found on the purchase ledger account, whereby the invoice for electricity was found to be recorded in the rent account. Select the type of error that has occurred by ticking the appropriate box in the table below.

Error	✓
Error of principle	
Unequal amounts error	
Error of omission	
Error of commission	

Task 5

Jones & Co pays its employees by BACS direct credit transfer every month and maintains a wages control account.

A summary of September's payroll transactions is shown below:

Gross wages	10,645
Employees' NI	1,230
Income tax	1,945
Employees' pension contributions	320
Employer's NI	1,450

Record the journal entries needed in the general ledger to:

(a) Journal to record the net wages paid to the employees

Account name		Debit £	Credit £
	▼		
	▼		

(b) Journal to record the HM Revenue and Customs liability

Account name		Debit £	Credit £
	▼		
	▼		

Picklist

Bank
HMRC control account
Wages control account
Wages expense account

Employee's contribute to their pension through their salary. For those employees who make these payments, the company contributes a further 6% of their gross wages.

Assuming all employees contribute to their pension, what is the amount that the company will be contributing in September? Record your answers in the journals below.

(c) Record the employee's pension contributions in the journal below

Account name		Debit £	Credit £
	▼		
	▼		

(d) Record the employer's pension contributions in the journal below (round your answer to the nearest pound)

Account name		Debit £	Credit £
	▼		
	▼		

(e) Transfer the employer's pension contributions (calculated in part (d)) to the Pension administrator control account

Account name		Debit £	Credit £
	▼		
	▼		

Picklist

Bank
Employees' NI
Employer's NI
HMRC control account
Income tax
Pension administrator control account
Trade union subs
Wages control account
Wages expense account

Task 6

Scriven Trading's trial balance was extracted and did not balance. The debit column of the trial balance totalled £139,406 and the credit column totalled £137,200.

(a) **What entry would be made in the suspense account to balance the trial balance?**

Account name	Amount £	Debit ✓	Credit ✓
Suspense			

In the following month Scriven Trading's initial trial balance includes a suspense account with a balance of £90.

The error has now been identified as arising from an incorrectly totalled net column in the sales day book shown below.

Sales day book

Date 20XX	Details	Invoice number	Total £	VAT £	Net £
30 Jul	Brancaster & Co	456	600	100	500
30 Jul	Norfolk Ales	457	570	95	475
30 Jul	Cley Cookery	458	816	136	680
	Totals		1,986	331	1,565

(b) **Record the journal entry needed in the general ledger to remove the incorrect entry made from the sales day book.**

Account name	Amount £	Debit ✓	Credit ✓
▼			

(c) **Record the journal entry needed in the general ledger to record the correct entry that should have been made from the sales day book.**

Account name	Amount £	Debit ✓	Credit ✓
▼			

(d) **Record the journal entry needed in the general ledger to remove the suspense account balance arising from the error in the sales day book.**

Account name	Amount £	Debit ✓	Credit ✓
▼			

Picklist

Balance b/f
Balance c/d
Sales
Suspense
Total
Trade receivables
VAT control

Task 7

The journal entries below have been prepared to correct an error.

Journal

Account name	Debit £	Credit £
Office expenses	2,455	
Suspense		2,455
Suspense	2,540	
Office expenses		2,540

Post the journal entries in the general ledger accounts below and show the balance carried down in the office expenses account.

Office expenses

Details	Amount £	Details	Amount £
Balance b/f	6,720	▼	
▼		▼	
▼			

Suspense

Details	Amount £	Details	Amount £
		Balance b/f	85
▼		▼	

Picklist

Balance b/f
Balance c/d
Office expenses
Suspense

Task 8

On 30 June Jones & Co extracted an initial trial balance which did not balance, and a suspense account with a debit balance of £1,690 was opened. On 1 July journal entries were prepared to correct the errors that had been found, and clear the suspense account. The list of balances in the initial trial balance, and the journal entries to correct the errors, are shown below.

Journal entries

Account name	Debit £	Credit £
Furniture and fittings		8,690
Suspense	8,690	
Furniture and fittings	9,680	
Suspense		9,680

Account name	Debit £	Credit £
Sales returns	350	
Suspense		350
Sales returns	350	
Suspense		350

Taking into account the journal entries, which will clear the suspense account, re-draft the trial balance by writing the figures in the debit or credit column. Do not enter your figures with decimal places in this task and do not enter a zero in the empty column.

	Balances extracted on 30 June £	Balances at 1 July	
		Debit £	Credit £
Machinery	15,240		
Furniture and fittings	8,690		
Inventory	11,765		
Bank (overdraft)	5,127		
Petty cash	100		
Sales ledger control	72,536		
Purchases ledger control	11,928		
VAT (owing to HM Revenue and Customs)	2,094		
Capital	80,000		
Sales	98,162		
Purchases	39,278		
Purchases returns	4,120		
Wages	22,855		
Sales returns	110		
Administration expenses	10,287		
Rent and rates	12,745		
Marketing expenses	3,289		
Irrecoverable debts	1,275		
Maintenance	1,571		
	Totals		

Task 9

The bank statement and cash book for May are shown below

Required

Check the bank statement against the cash book and enter:

- Any transactions into the cash book as needed
- The cash book balance carried down at 31 May and brought down at 1 June.

Enter dates in the format "XX Dec".

Bank statement

Date 20XX	Details	Paid out £	Paid in £	Balance £
01 May	Balance b/f			900 D
02 May	Counter credit		4,250	3,350 C
02 May	Cheque 00793	250		3,100 C
05 May	Cheque 00795	1,300		1,800 C
08 May	Direct debit: PinkGreen Ltd	200		1,600 C
12 May	Direct debit: Maple Leaf & Co	425		1,175 C
18 May	Counter credit		6,400	7,575 C
21 May	Counter credit		2,475	10,050 C
22 May	Bank interest		15	10,065 C
23 May	Bank charges	30		10,035 C
30 May	Direct debit: Oak Insurance	130		9,905 C

D=Debit C=Credit

(a) Cash book

Date 20XX	Details	Bank £	Date 20XX	Cheque number	Details	Bank £
02 May	Parks & Co	4,250	01 May		Balance bf	900
18 May	Flower Bulb Co	6,400	01 May	00793	Greenways	250
20 May	Mowaway ltd	2,475	01 May	00794	Blossom & co	2,100
22 May	▼		01 May	00795	White Pines	1,300
					▼	
					▼	
					▼	
					▼	
					▼	
	▼				▼	

Picklist

Balance b/d
Balance c/d
Bank charges
Bank interest
Blossom & co
Greenways
Maple Leaf & Co
Mowaway Ltd
Oak insurance
PinkGreen Ltd
White Pines

(b) Calculate the difference between the bank statement and the cash book balance as at 31 May.

	£
Balance on the bank statement as at 31 May	
Balance on the cash book as at 31 May	
Difference	

(c) Which of the following items would need to be entered into the bank reconciliation in order for the bank statement and the cash book to balance at 31 May.

Cheque to Blossom & Co for £2,100	
Bank interest of £15	
Credit from Mowaway Ltd of £2,475	

Task 10

Below is the bank statement dated 30 April

Date 20XX	Details	Paid out £	Paid in £	Balance £
01 Apr	Balance b/f			450 C
02 Apr	Counter credit		7,125	7,575 C
02 Apr	Bank charges	45		7,530 C
05 Apr	Cheque 0077	1,260		6,270C
10 Apr	Counter credit		435	6,705 C
15 Apr	Direct debit	2,700		4,005C
22 Apr	Counter credit		2,330	6,335 C
28 Apr	L Barlow (payroll payment)	1,200		5,135 C
28 Apr	J Lowenstein (payroll payment)	845		4,290 C

D = Debit C = Credit

Required

(a) Complete the missing entries for the cash book below.

(b) On 30 April 20XX, a further three cheques were raised to pay suppliers. Ensure that the cashbook has been updated for these transactions. Put the cashbook totals in and ensure balance carried down has been calculated.

Details	Amount £
LTC Limited 0078	3,400
Gaffney & Co 0079	950
Bubble Corp 0080	245

Cash book

Date 20XX	Details	Bank £	Date 20XX	Cheque number	Details	Bank £
01 Apr	Balance b/d	450	01 Apr	0077	Joyful Ltd	1,260
02 Apr	Scrape & Co	7,125	15 Apr	DD	Rent	2,700
10 Apr	Eric & Sons Ltd	435				
22 Apr	B Fay	2,330				
30 Apr	Bake Sale plc	1,450				

Picklist

Balance b/d
Balance c/d
Bank charges
Bank interest
Bubble Corp
Gaffney & Co
Joyful Ltd
LTC Limited
Payroll
Rent

(c) Complete the bank reconciliation identifying the reconciling items

Bank reconciliation statement	£
Balance per bank statement	
Add:	
 ▼	
Total to add	
Less:	
▼	
▼	
▼	
Total to subtract	
Balance as per cash book	

Picklist

Bake Sale plc
Balance b/d
Balance c/d
Bank charges
Bank interest
Bubble Corp
Eric & Sons
Gaffney & Co
Joyful Ltd
LTC Limited
Payroll
Rent
Scrape & Co

BPP PRACTICE ASSESSMENT 2
BOOKKEEPING CONTROLS

ANSWERS

Bookkeeping Controls
BPP practice assessment 2

Task 1

(a)

Payment Method	Reduce funds on the date of payment ✓	Reduce funds at a later date ✓
Credit card		✓
Cash withdrawal from the bank account	✓	
BACS direct credit	✓	
Cheque		✓
CHAPS	✓	

The credit card statement will be affected in the first instance, so the current account will not be affected until the credit statement is paid at a later date. Cash is withdrawn from the bank account immediately. The BACS direct credit leaves the payer's account immediately and is usually received within 24 hours by the payee. Cheques affect the bank account when the payee presents them, which may take several days or weeks. CHAPS has an immediate affect on the bank account once it has been processed by the payer.

(b)

Situation	Payment method
Payment of an invoice to a supplier where goods were purchased on credit. The payment is due today and is for £1,300	Faster payment
Purchasing tea and coffee supplies for the office from the local supermarket	Cash
Ordering new printer paper online	Debit card
Payment of local business rates on a monthly basis for the same value each month (£250)	Direct Debit
Payment of legal fees to the company's solicitor for general business advice (£550)	Debit card

The final option in the table could be paid by cheque, but many businesses use debit cards for smaller payments. A debit card is relevant here as it is a quick and suitable for smaller monetary transactions.

(c)

Error in the general ledger	Error disclosed by the trial balance ✓	Error NOT disclosed by the trial balance ✓
Making a transposition error in the debit entry from the journal in the general ledger but not in the credit entry	✓	
Recording a sale to a customer for £75 cash (no VAT) as £57 in both the cash account and the sales account		✓
Recording a payment for a cash purchase (no VAT) in the trade payables column of the cash book		✓
Recording discount allowed to a customer on the debit side of the discount allowed account and the debit side of the sales ledger control account	✓	
Recording a payment to a supplier on the credit side of the supplier's purchases ledger account		✓
Recording a sales return by debiting the sales ledger control account and crediting the sales returns account		✓

(d)

	✓
Making a transposition error in the debit entry from the journal in the general ledger but not in the credit entry	
Recording a sale to a customer for £75 cash (no VAT) as £57 in both the cash account and the sales account	
Recording a payment for a cash purchase (no VAT) in the trade payables column of the cash book	
Recording discount allowed to a customer on the debit side of the discount allowed account and the debit side of the sales ledger control account	
Recording a payment to a supplier on the credit side of the supplier's purchases ledger account	
Recording a sales return by debiting the sales ledger control account and crediting the sales returns account	✓

Task 2

(a)

Details	Amount £	Debit ✓	Credit ✓
VAT owing to HM Revenue and Customs at 1 March	2,300		✓
VAT total in the sales daybook	5,320		✓
VAT total in the sales returns daybook	410	✓	
VAT total in the purchases daybook	3,100	✓	
VAT total in the discounts allowed daybook	250	✓	
VAT total in the discounts received daybook	170		✓
VAT total in the cash book for cash sales	900		✓
VAT payment sent to HM Revenue and Customs	2,300	✓	

(b)

Amount £	Debit ✓	Credit ✓
2,630		✓

(c)

Account name	Amount £	Debit ✓	Credit ✓
Irrecoverable debts	500	✓	
VAT	100	✓	
Sales ledger control	600		✓

Task 3

(a)

VAT control

Details	Amount £	Details	Amount £
Sales returns	560	Sales	10,710
Purchases	3,255	Purchases returns	217
		Cash sales	168

(b) The answer is Jones and Co owe HMRC £7,280 (this is the carried down figure as seen in the workings below)

Working:

Details	Amount £	Details	Amount £
Sales returns	560	Sales	10,710
Purchases	3,255	Purchases returns	217
		Cash sales	168
Balance c/d	**7,280**		
	11,095		11,095
		Balance b/d	**7,280**

(c)

	✓
The VAT control account is used to establish any balance due to or reclaimable from HMRC	✓
Payments to HMRC in respect of VAT owed are debited to the cash book and credited to the VAT control account	
The balance b/d on the VAT control account is the amount owed to (credit balance) or refundable by (debit balance) HMRC	✓
A return on sales (where VAT is charged) increases the VAT liability in the VAT control account	

Task 4

(a)

£	12,710

(b)

£	110

(c)

Reasons	✓
A payment from a customer was allocated against the wrong customer	
Discounts allowed were not entered in the sales ledger control account	
Goods sold were entered twice in the sales ledger control account	
Goods returned were omitted from the sales ledger.	✓

(d)

Error	✓
Error of principle	
Unequal amounts error	
Error of omission	
Error of commission	✓

Error of commission is where the item has been recorded in the right type of account (in this case, that of the Statement of Profit and Loss) but the wrong account has been used (in this case rent instead of electricity. It is not an error of principle (it would have had to been recorded onto the Statement of Financial Position, the wrong type of account). The amounts are equal (therefore not an error of unequal amounts). The item has been recorded therefore it is not an error of omission.

Task 5

(a)

Account name	Debit £	Credit £
Wages control account	7,150	
Bank		7,150

(b)

Account name	Debit £	Credit £
Wages control account	4,625	
HMRC control account		4,625

(c)

Account name	Debit £	Credit £
Wages control account	320	
Pension administrator control account		320

(d)

Account name	Debit £	Credit £
Wages expense account	639	
Wages control account		639

(e)

Account name	Debit £	Credit £
Wages control account	639	
Pension administrator control account		639

Task 6

(a)

Account name	Amount £	Debit ✓	Credit ✓
Suspense	2,206		✓

(b)

Account name	Amount £	Debit ✓	Credit ✓
Sales	1,565	✓	

(c)

Account name	Amount £	Debit ✓	Credit ✓
Sales	1,655		✓

(d)

Account name	Amount £	Debit ✓	Credit ✓
Suspense	90	✓	

Picklist

Balance b/f
Balance c/d
Suspense
Total
Trade receivables
VAT

Task 7

Office expenses

Details	Amount £	Details	Amount £
Balance b/f	6,720	Suspense	2,540
Suspense	2,455	Balance c/d	6,635
	9,175		9,175

Suspense

Details	Amount £	Details	Amount £
		Balance b/f	85
Office expenses	2,540	Office expenses	2,455
	2,540		2,540

Task 8

	Balances extracted on 30 June £	Balances at 1 July	
		Debit £	Credit £
Machinery	15,240	15,240	
Furniture and fittings	8,690	9,680	
Inventory	11,765	11,765	
Bank (overdraft)	5,127		5,127
Petty cash	100	100	
Sales ledger control	72,536	72,536	
Purchases ledger control	11,928		11,928
VAT (owing to HM Revenue and Customs)	2,094		2,094
Capital	80,000		80,000
Sales	98,162		98,162
Purchases	39,278	39,278	
Purchases returns	4,120		4,120
Wages	22,855	22,855	
Sales returns	110	810	
Administration expenses	10,287	10,287	
Rent and rates	12,745	12,745	
Marketing expenses	3,289	3,289	
Irrecoverable debts	1,275	1,275	
Maintenance	1,571	1,571	
	Totals	201,431	201,431

Task 9

Bank statement

Date 20XX	Details	Paid out £	Paid in £	Balance £
01 May	Balance b/f			900 D
02 May	Counter credit		4,250	3,350 C
02 May	Cheque 00793	250		3,100 C
05 May	Cheque 00795	1,300		1,800 C
08 May	Direct debit: PinkGreen Ltd	200		1,600 C
12 May	Direct debit: Maple Leaf & Co	425		1,175 C
18 May	Counter credit		6,400	7,575 C
21 May	Counter credit		2,475	10,050 C
22 May	Bank interest		15	10,065 C
23 May	Bank charges	30		10,035 C
30 May	Direct debit: Oak Insurance	130		9,905 C

D=Debit C=Credit

(a) Cash book

Date 20XX	Details	Bank £	Date 20XX	Cheque number	Details	Bank £
02 May	Parks & Co	4,250	01 May		Balance bf	900
18 May	Flower Bulb Co	6,400	01 May	00793	Greenways	250
20 May	Mowaway ltd	2,475	01 May	00794	Blossom & co	2,100
22 May	Bank interest	15	01 May	00795	White Pines	1,300
			08 May	DD	PinkGreen Ltd	200
			12 May	DD	Maple Leaf & Co	425
			23 May		Bank charges	30
			30 May	DD	Oak Insurance	130
			31 May		Balance c/d	7,805
		13,140				13,140
1 Jun	Balance b/d	7,805				

(b)

	£
Balance on the bank statement as at 31 May	9,905
Balance on the cash book as at 31 May	7,805
Difference	2,100

(c)

Cheque to Blossom & Co for £2,100	✓
Bank interest of £15	
Credit from Mowaway Ltd of £2,475	

Task 10

Cash book

Date 20XX	Details	Bank £	Date 20XX	Cheque number	Details	Bank £
01 Apr	Balance b/d	450	01 Apr	0077	Joyful Ltd	1,260
02 Apr	Scrape & Co	7,125	15 Apr	DD	Rent	2,700
10 Apr	Eric & Sons Ltd	435	02 Apr		Bank charges	45
22 Apr	B Fay	2,330	28 Apr		Payroll	1,200
30 Apr	Bake Sale plc	1,450	28 Apr		Payroll	845
			30 Apr	0078	LTC Ltd	3,400
			30 Apr	0079	Gaffney & Co	950
			30 Apr	0080	Bubble Corp	245
			30 Apr		Balance c/d	1,145
		11,790				11,790
	Balance b/d	1,145				

Bank reconciliation statement	
Balance per bank statement	4,290
Add:	
Bake Sale plc	1,450
Total to add	1,450
Less:	
LTC Ltd	3,400
Gaffney & Co	950
Bubble Corporation	245
Total to subtract	4,595
Balance as per cash book	1,145

BPP PRACTICE ASSESSMENT 3
BOOKKEEPING CONTROLS

Time allowed: 2 hours

Bookkeeping Controls
BPP practice assessment 3

Each task is independent. You will not need to refer to your answers to previous tasks.

Read every task carefully to make sure you understand what is required.

Where the date is relevant, it is given in the task data.

Both minus signs and brackets can be used to indicate negative numbers **unless** task instructions say otherwise.

You must use a full stop to indicate a decimal point. For example, write 100.57 **not** 100,57 **or** 100 57.

You may use a comma to indicate a number in the thousands, but you don't have to. For example, 10000 and 10,000 are both OK.

Other indicators are not compatible with the computer-marked system.

Complete all 10 tasks.

You are employed by the business, Pratesh Supplies Limited, as a bookkeeper.

- Pratesh Supplies Limited uses a manual accounting system.

- Double entry takes place in the general ledger. Individual accounts of trade receivables and trade payables are kept in the sales and purchases ledgers as subsidiary accounts.

- The cash book and petty cash book should be treated as part of the double entry system unless the task instructions state otherwise.

- The VAT rate is 20%.

Task 1

(a) **Identify the effect the different payment methods have on the bank balance. Please tick the appropriate box in each case.**

Payment Method	Reduce funds on the date of payment ✓	Reduce funds at a later date ✓
Credit card		
Bank draft		
Cheque		
CHAPS		
Direct Debit		

(b) Select the most appropriate method of payment for the following transactions from the picklist below

Situation	Payment method
Purchase of a new computer from Laptops Limited, which is an online discount supplier	
Invoice payment to a supplier who requires immediate payment today for £2,400	
Payment of the payroll for the month of March to employees	
Payment of rent on a new office on a monthly basis (£2,450)	
Purchase of a new warehouse for the business (£125,000)	

Picklist

BACS direct credit
Cash
CHAPS
Cheque
Credit card
Direct Debit
Faster payment
Standing order

(c) Select which TWO of the following statements are correct by ticking the appropriate option

Error	✓
When a payment is made using a credit card, the money leaves the bank account immediately	
Standing orders are regular payments set up by the payer	
A bank draft can be cancelled by the payer after it has been issued	
Money leaves the payer's bank account immediately upon issuance of a bank draft	

(d) Show which error is an error of original entry by ticking the appropriate option

Error in the general ledger	✓
Writing in the balance on the office stationery account incorrectly	
Recording a purchase from a credit supplier for £5,000 (no VAT) as £500 in both the purchases and the purchases ledger control accounts	
Recording a receipt from a credit customer in the cash sales account	
Recording a credit note from a supplier on the debit side of the purchases ledger control account and the debit side of the purchases returns account	

Task 2

Show whether the errors below will cause an imbalance in the trial balance by ticking the appropriate column.

Error in the general ledger	Error disclosed by the trial balance ✓	Error NOT disclosed by the trial balance ✓
For a cash sale of £340 (no VAT), recording the amount as £34 in the cash book		
Recording £50 discount received on the credit side of PLCA and the debit side of the discount received account		
Recording a purchase from a supplier for £180 including VAT as £180 in the PLCA and purchases accounts and £30 in the VAT account		
Making a transposition error when transferring a balance from the ledger account to the trial balance		
Recording a payment from a credit customer for £200 in the debit side of the sales ledger account		

Task 3

The following is an extract from the bank statement for March. The two staff members are paid on the closest working day to the 15th of each month.

The cash book and bank reconciliation statement for March have not been finalised.

Required

(a) **Complete the cash book for any missing entries during March, including the balance brought down at 1 April 20XX**

Date 20XX	Details	Paid out £	Paid in £	Balance £
01 Mar	Balance b/f			7,250 C
02 Mar	Cheque 820	4,450		2,800 C
02 Mar	Cheque 821	2,100		700 C
09 Mar	Counter credit: Jeffersons & Co		750	1,450 C
12 Mar	Direct debit: Carter insurance	990		460 C
13 Mar	K Brown	1,800		1,340 D
13 Mar	J Patel	1,600		2,940 D
22 Mar	Counter credit: Clinton & Clinton		9,250	6,310 C
28 Mar	Bank charges	100		6,210 C

D = Debit C = Credit

The cash book as at 31 March is shown below:

Cash book

Date 20XX	Details	Bank £	Date 20XX	Cheque number	Details	Bank £
01 Mar	Balance b/f	7,250	01 Mar	820	Nixon Ltd	4,450
02 Mar	Jeffersons & Co	750	01 Mar	821	Roosevelts	2,100
22 Mar	Clinton & Clinton	9,250	02 Mar	822	GWB LLP	1,750
30 Mar	Garfield & Son	1,450			▼	
30 Mar	Adams	4,600			▼	
					▼	
					▼	
					▼	
	▼					

Picklist

Adams
Balance b/d
Balance c/d
Bank charges
Bank interest
Carter insurance
Clinton & Clinton
Garfield & Son
GWB LLP
J Patel
Jeffersons & Co
K Brown
Nixon Ltd
Roosevelts

(b) **Complete the bank reconciliation statement as at 31 March.**

Note. Do not make any entries in the shaded boxes.

Bank reconciliation statement as at 31 March 20XX	£
Balance per bank statement	
Add:	
▼	
▼	
Total to add	
Less:	
▼	
▼	
Total to subtract	
Balance as per cash book	

Picklist

Adams
Balance b/d
Balance c/d
Bank charges
Bank interest
Clinton & Clinton
Garfield & Son
GWB LLP
Jeffersons & Co
J Patel
K Brown
Nixon Ltd
Roosevelts

(c) **Refer to the cash book in (a) and check that the bank statement has been correctly reconciled by calculating:**

- **The balance carried down**

- **The total of each of the bank columns after the balance carried down has been recorded.**

Balance carried down £	Bank column totals £

Task 4

This is a customer's account in the sales ledger.

Worcester Building Co

Date 20XX	Details	Amount £	Date 20XX	Details	Amount £
01 Jan	Invoice 482	1,400	15 Jan	Payment	1,350
15 Feb	Invoice 495	785	22 Feb	Credit Note 24	509
22 Mar	Invoice 522	250			

(a) **Calculate the amount outstanding by Worcester Building Co as at 31 March**

The customer has now ceased trading as of 15 April owing the amount outstanding which **includes** VAT. Enter your answer in the box provided

£ [   ]

(b) **Record the journal entries needed in the general ledger to write off the net amount and the VAT as at 30 April. Use the picklist provided.**

	Amount £	Debit ✓	Credit ✓
▼			
▼			
▼			

Picklist

Irrecoverable debts
Sales ledger control
VAT control

(c) **In the next quarter, the VAT control account has debit entries amount to £4,690 and credit entries amount to £3,460**

The following transactions have not yet been recorded in the VAT control account:

- VAT total of £600 in the purchases daybook

- VAT of £180 on an irrecoverable debt written off

- Payment made to HMRC of £1,200 in respect of VAT payable for the previous quarter

Complete the VAT control account below, including the balance c/d at the end of the month

VAT Control

Account name		Amount £	Account name		Credit ✓
	▼		Balance b/f		
	▼			▼	
	▼			▼	
	▼				

Picklist

Balance c/d
Bank
Irrecoverable debt
Purchases
Sales
Sales ledger control

Task 5

Pratesh Supplies Limited pays its employees by BACS direct credit transfer every month and maintains a wages control account.

A summary of last month's payroll transactions is shown below:

	£
Gross wages	10,260
Employees' NI	925
Income tax	2,335
Employees' pension contributions	780
Employer's pension contribution	900
Employer's NI	1,300

BPP
LEARNING MEDIA

Record the journal entries needed in the general ledger to:

(a)   Journal to record wages expense

Account name		Debit £	Credit £
	▾		
	▾		

(b)   Journal to record the HM Revenue and Customs liability

Account name		Debit £	Credit £
	▾		
	▾		

(c)   Journal to record the pension administrator liability

Account name		Debit £	Credit £
	▾		
	▾		

Picklist

Bank
Employees' NI
Employer's NI
HM Revenue and Customs
Income tax
Net wages
Pension administrator
Wages control
Wages expense

Task 6

This is a summary of transactions with customers during the month of August.

(a) **Show whether each entry will be a debit or credit in the sales ledger control account in the general ledger.**

Sales ledger control account

Details	Amount £	Debit ✓	Credit ✓
Balance of receivables at 1 August	15,100		
Goods sold on credit	28,375		
Payments received from credit customers	16,450		
Discounts allowed	425		
Goods returned by credit customers	900		

(b) **What will be the balance brought down on 1 September on the above account?**

£ [   ]

(c) **The following debit balances were in the sales ledger on 31 August.**

	£
Kendrick plc	7,300
Askwith Ltd	4,680
Raston Permanent Ltd	5,461
Biomass plc	1,400
Nistral plc	2,009
Larkmead & Co	4,650

Complete the following table to reconcile the balances shown above with the sales ledger control account balance you have calculated in part (b).

Sales ledger control account balance as at 31 August	
Total of sales ledger accounts as at 31 August	
Difference	

(d) What may have caused the difference you calculated in part (c)?

	✓
Goods returned may have been omitted from the sales ledger	
Discounts allowed may have been omitted from the sales ledger	
Goods returned may have been entered in the sales ledger twice	
Sales invoices may have been entered in the sales ledger twice	

It is important to reconcile the sales ledger control account on a regular basis.

(e) Which ONE of the following statements is true?

	✓
Reconciliation of the sales ledger control account assures managers that the amount showing as outstanding from customers is correct.	
Reconciliation of the sales ledger control account assures managers that the amount showing as outstanding to suppliers is correct.	
Reconciliation of the sales ledger control account will show if a purchases invoice has been omitted from the purchases ledger.	
Reconciliation of the sales ledger control account will show if a sales invoice has been omitted from the purchases ledger.	

Task 7

A credit purchase return of £1,170 has been entered in the accounting records as £1,710. (Ignore VAT.)

(a) Using the picklist below, record the journal entries needed in the general ledger to remove the incorrect entry.

Account name		Amount £	Debit ✓	Credit ✓
	▼			
	▼			

(b) Record the journal entries needed in the general ledger to record the correct entry.

Account name	Amount £	Debit ✓	Credit ✓
▼			
▼			

Picklist

Bank
Cash
Purchases ledger control
Purchases returns
Purchases returns day book
Suspense
Trade payables

(c) Show ONE reason for producing the trial balance.

	✓
To detect fraud	
To check that double entry has been performed correctly	
To comply with the statutory requirement	
To save time	

Task 8

The bank statement and cash book for June are shown below

Required

(a) Check the bank statement against the cash book and enter:

- **Any transactions into the cash book as needed using the picklist provided**
- **The cash book balance carried down at 10 June**

Enter dates in the format "XX Jun".

Bank statement

Date 20XX	Details	Paid out £	Paid in £	Balance £
01 Jun	Balance b/f			1,250 C
02 Jun	Counter credit: Jonas Limited		5,000	6,250 C
02 Jun	Direct Debit: Waterville DC	250		6,000 C
03 Jun	Direct debit: Ocksan CC	300		5,700 C
03 Jun	Counter credit: Nadia & Co		3,250	8,950 C
03 Jun	Cheque 0123	2,500		6,450 C
06 Jun	Cheque 0125	750		5,700 C
07 Jun	Direct debit: Billymots Insurance	125		5,575 C
09 Jun	Bank interest		10	5,585 C
09 Jun	Bank charges	26		5559 C
10 Jun	Counter credit: Jakir Ltd		850	6,409 C

D=Debit C=Credit

Cash book

Date 20XX	Details	Bank £	Date 20XX	Cheque number	Details	Bank £
01 Jun	Balance b/f	1,250	01 Jun	0123	Freddo Ltd	2,500
02 Jun	Jonas Limited	5,000	01 Jun	0124	Quicksand	1,200
03 Jun	Nadia & Co	3,250	01 Jun	0125	New & Co	750
10 Jun	Brilliant Ltd	4,500	01 Jun	0126	Wilmers	650
	▼		02 Jun	DD	Waterville DC	250
	▼				▼	
					▼	
					▼	
					▼	

Picklist

Balance c/d
Bank charges
Bank interest
Billymots Insurance
Jakir Ltd
Nadia & Co
Ocksan CC
Waterville DC

(b) **Once the cash book has been updated, identify which of the following would be reconciling items on the bank reconciliation at 10 June. Make your selection by ticking the appropriate option(s).**

	✓
Quicksand £1,200	
Wilmers £650	
Bank interest £10	
Brilliant Ltd £4,500	
Jakir Ltd £850	

Task 9

On 30 June Pratesh Supplies extracted an initial trial balance which did not balance, and a suspense account with a credit balance of £420 was opened. On 1 July journal entries were prepared to correct the errors that had been found, and clear the suspense account. The journal entries to correct the errors, and the list of balances in the initial trial balance, are shown below.

Journal entries

Account name	Debit £	Credit £
Purchases ledger control		507
Suspense	507	
Purchases ledger control		507
Suspense	507	

Account name	Debit £	Credit £
Heat and light		1,056
Suspense	1,056	
Heat and light	1,650	
Suspense		1,650

Taking into account the journal entries, which will clear the suspense account, re-draft the trial balance by writing the figures in the debit or credit column. Do not enter your figures with decimal places in this task and do not enter a zero in the empty column.

	Balances extracted on 30 June £	Balances at 1 July	
		Debit £	Credit £
Motor vehicles	13,920		
Furniture and fittings	9,208		
Inventory	10,129		
Cash at bank	673		
Petty cash	250		
Sales ledger control	7,832		
Purchases ledger control	4,292		
VAT (owing to HM Revenue and Customs)	1,029		
Capital	10,000		
Sales	89,125		
Purchases	35,268		
Purchases returns	1,092		
Wages	18,279		
Marketing expenses	1,290		
Office expenses	3,287		
Rent and rates	2,819		
Heat and light	1,056		
Irrecoverable debts	127		
Motor expenses	1,820		
Totals			

Task 10

On 28 February a trial balance was extracted and did not balance. The debit column totaled £245,100 and the credit column totaled £244,535.

(a) **What entry would be made in the suspense account to balance the trial balance?**

Account name	Amount £	Debit ✓	Credit ✓
Suspense			

The journal entries to correct all the bookkeeping errors, and a list of balances as they appear in the trial balance, are shown below

Account name	Debit ✓	Credit ✓
Suspense	1,200	
Bank		1,200
Advertising	1,200	
Bank		1,200

Account name	Debit ✓	Credit ✓
Office supplies	785	
Suspense		785
Suspense	150	
Bank interest		150

(b) **Complete the table below to show:**

- the balance of each account after the journal entries have been recorded
- whether each balance will be a debit or credit entry in the trial balance.

List of balances

Account name	Original balance £	New balance £	Debit ✓	Credit ✓
Office supplies	800			
Bank (debit)	4,500			
Advertising	1,960			
Bank interest received	450			

On 30 April a partially prepared trial balance for Pratesh Supplies new subsidiary company, Tarka Limited, had debit balances totalling £172,600 and credit balances totalling £168,400. The accounts below have not yet been entered into the trial balance.

(c) **Complete the table below to show whether each balance will be a debit or credit entry in the trial balance.**

Account name	Balance £	Debit ✓	Credit ✓
Bank Loan	4,600		
VAT control (owed to HMRC)	3,496		
Fixed assets, fixtures & fitting	2,000		
Rent paid	1,896		

(d) **What will be the totals of each column of the trial balance after the balances in (c) have been entered?**

Account name	Debit ✓	Credit ✓
Totals		

....

BPP PRACTICE ASSESSMENT 3
BOOKKEEPING CONTROLS

ANSWERS

Bookkeeping Controls
BPP practice assessment 3

Task 1

(a)

Payment Method	Reduce funds on the date of payment ✓	Reduce funds at a later date ✓
Credit card		✓
Bank draft	✓	
Cheque		✓
CHAPS	✓	
Direct Debit	✓	

(b)

Situation	Payment method
Purchase of a new computer from Laptops Limited, which is an online discount supplier	Credit card
Invoice payment to a supplier who requires immediate payment today for £2,400	Faster payment
Payment of the payroll for the month of March to employees	BACS direct credit
Payment of rent on a new office on a monthly basis (£2,450)	Standing order
Purchase of a new warehouse for the business (£125,000)	CHAPS

(c)

Error	✓
When a payment is made using a credit card, the money leaves the bank account immediately	
Standing orders are regular payments set up by the payer	✓
A bank draft can be cancelled by the payer after it has been issued	
Money leaves the payer's bank account immediately upon issuance of a bank draft	✓

(d)

Error in the general ledger	✓
Writing in the balance on the office stationery account incorrectly	
Recording a purchase from a credit supplier for £5,000 (no VAT) as £500 in both the purchases and the purchases ledger control accounts	✓
Recording a receipt from a credit customer in the cash sales account	
Recording a credit note from a supplier on the debit side of the purchases ledger control account and the debit side of the purchases returns account	

Task 2

Error in the general ledger	Error disclosed by the trial balance ✓	Error NOT disclosed by the trial balance ✓
For a cash sale of £340 (no VAT), recording the amount as £34 in the cash book		✓
Recording £50 discount received on the credit side of PLCA and the debit side of the discount received account		✓
Recording a purchase from a supplier for £180 including VAT as £180 in the PLCA and purchases accounts and £30 in the VAT account	✓	
Making a transposition error when transferring a balance from the ledger account to the trial balance	✓	
Recording a payment from a credit customer for £200 in the debit side of the sales ledger account		✓

Task 3

(a)

Date 20XX	Details	Bank £	Date 20XX	Cheque number	Details	Bank £
01 Mar	Balance b/f	7,250	01 Mar	820	Nixon Ltd	4,450
02 Mar	Jeffersons & Co	750	01 Mar	821	Roosevelts	2,100
22 Mar	Clinton & Clinton	9,250	02 Mar	822	GWB LLP	1,750
30 Mar	Garfield & Son	1,450	12 Mar	DD	Carter insurance	990
30 Mar	Adams	4,600	13 Mar	Payroll	K Brown	1,800
			13 Mar	Payroll	J Patel	1,600
			22 Mar		Bank charges	100
			31 Mar		Balance c/d	10,510
		23,300				23,300
1 Apr	Balance b/d	10,510				

(b)

Bank reconciliation statement	£
Balance per bank statement	6,210
Add:	
Garfield & Son	1,450
Adams	4,600
Total to add	6,050
Less:	
GWB LLP	1,750
Total to subtract	1,750
Balance as per cash book	10,510

(c)

Balance carried down £	Bank column totals £
10,510	23,300

Task 4

(a) The answer is £576 (1,400+785+250-1,350-509)

(b)

Account name	Amount £	Debit ✓	Credit ✓
Irrecoverable debts	480	✓	
VAT control	96	✓	
Sales ledger control	576		✓

(c)

Account name	Amount £	Account name	Credit ✓
Purchases	4,690	Balance b/f	1,200
Purchases	600	Sales	3,460
Irrecoverable debt	180	Balance c/d	2,010
Payment	1,200		
	6,670		6,670

Task 5

(a)

Account name	Debit £	Credit £
Wages expense (900+10,260+1,300)	12,460	
Wages control		12,460

(b)

Account name	Debit £	Credit £
Wages control (2,335+925+1,300)	4,560	
HMRC		4,560

234

(c)

Account name	Debit £	Credit £
Wages control (900+780)	1,680	
Pension administrator		1,680

Task 6

(a) **Sales ledger control account**

Details	Amount £	Debit ✓	Credit ✓
Balance of receivables at 1 August	15,100	✓	
Goods sold on credit	28,375	✓	
Payments received from credit customers	16,450		✓
Discounts allowed	425		✓
Goods returned by credit customers	900		✓

(b)

£	25,700

(c)

	£
Sales ledger control account balance as at 31 August	25,700
Total of sales ledger accounts as at 31 August	25,500
Difference	200

(d) The correct answer is: Goods returned may have been entered in the sales ledger twice

(e) The correct answer is: Reconciliation of the sales ledger control account assures managers that the amount showing as outstanding from customers is correct

Task 7

(a)

Account name	Amount £	Debit ✓	Credit ✓
Purchases returns	1,710	✓	
Purchases ledger control	1,710		✓

(b)

Account name	Amount £	Debit ✓	Credit ✓
Purchases ledger control	1,170	✓	
Purchases returns	1,170		✓

(c)

	✓
To detect fraud	
To check that double entry has been performed correctly	✓
To comply with the statutory requirement	
To save time	

Task 8

(a)

Date 20XX	Details	Bank £	Date 20XX	Cheque number	Details	Bank £
01 Jun	Balance b/f	1,250	01 Jun	0123	Freddo Ltd	2,500
02 Jun	Jonas Limited	5,000	01 Jun	0124	Quicksand	1,200
03 Jun	Nadia & Co	3,250	01 Jun	0125	New & Co	750
10 Jun	Brilliant Ltd	4,500	01 Jun	0126	Wilmers	650
09 Jun	**Bank interest**	**10**	02 Jun	DD	Waterville DC	250
10 Jun	**Jakir Ltd**	**850**	03 Jun	DD	Ocksan CC	300
			07 Jun	DD	**Billymots Insurance**	125
			09 Jun		**Bank charges**	26
			10 Jun		Balance c/d	9,059
		14,860				14,860

(b)

Reconciling Item	✓
Quicksand £1,200	✓
Wilmers £650	✓
Bank interest £10	
Brilliant Ltd £4,500	✓
Jakir Ltd £850	

Task 9

	Balances extracted on 30 June £	Balances at 1 July	
		Debit £	Credit £
Motor vehicles	13,920	13,920	
Furniture and fittings	9,208	9,208	
Inventory	10,129	10,129	
Cash at bank	673	673	
Petty cash	250	250	
Sales ledger control	7,832	7,832	
Purchases ledger control	4,292		5,306
VAT (owing to HM Revenue and Customs)	1,029		1,029
Capital	10,000		10,000
Sales	89,125		89,125
Purchases	35,268	35,268	
Purchases returns	1,092		1,092
Wages	18,279	18,279	
Marketing expenses	1,290	1,290	
Office expenses	3,287	3,287	
Rent and rates	2,819	2,819	
Heat and light	1,056	1,650	
Irrecoverable debts	127	127	
Motor expenses	1,820	1,820	
	Totals	106,552	106,552

Task 10

(a)

Account name	Amount £	Debit ✓	Credit ✓
Suspense	565		✓

(b)

Account name	Original balance £	New balance £	Debit ✓	Credit ✓
Office supplies	800	1,585	✓	
Bank (debit)	4,500	2,100	✓	
Advertising	1,960	3,160	✓	
Bank interest received	450	600		✓

(c)

	Balance £	Debit ✓	Credit ✓
Bank Loan	4,600		✓
VAT control (owed to HMRC)	3,496		✓
Fixed assets, fixtures & fitting	2,000	✓	
Rent paid	1,896	✓	

(d)

Account name	Debit ✓	Credit ✓
Totals	176,496	176,496

Notes

Notes

Notes

Notes

Notes

Notes

Notes